SALVATION ON THE
SMALL SCREEN

SALVATION ON THE SMALL SCREEN

24 HOURS OF CHRISTIAN TELEVISION

NADIA BOLZ-WEBER

SEABURY BOOKS
New York

Cover design by Rob Carmichael
Cover photos by Janet Loo
Interior design by John Eagleson

Library of Congress Cataloging-in-Publication Data

Bolz-Weber, Nadia.
    Salvation on the small screen? : 24 hours of Christian television / by Nadia Bolz-Weber.
      p.   cm.
    ISBN 978-1-59627-086-2 (pbk.)
    1. Television in religion – United States. 2. Television broadcasting –
Religious aspects – Christianity.   I. Title.
BV656.3.B65 2008
269′.260973 – dc22

                                                            2008024254

Seabury Books
An imprint of Church Publishing Incorporated
445 Fifth Avenue
New York, NY 10016
www.churchpublishing.org

5 4 3 2 1

For Matthew,
my long-suffering husband,
without whom I would not have
the most beautiful things in my life

Contents

SALVATION ON THE SMALL SCREEN

Introduction

To say that Christian television is "not my thing" doesn't even get close. Christian music, Christian bookstores, Christian television, pretty much any aspect of what some call "the Christian-Industrial Complex," is "not my thing." Meanwhile, I have a blog called *Sarcastic Lutheran*, I am married to a Lutheran pastor, am involved in the start of a new postmodern, urban Christian community and, God willing, will soon be ordained to the office of Word and Sacrament ministry in the Lutheran Church, all of which is to say, I'm pretty Christian.

I'm not alone. Simply stated, there are two Christianities in America. (There are countless more Christianities in America that do not fit into the following categories, but humor me.) Group A are Christian and typically still are part of the dominant culture. They read books from the *New York Times* bestseller list, watch the Simpsons, and listen to pop music. These folks are more likely to belong to the moderate-to-progressive "mainline" denominations. Group B are also Christian, and they read books and watch TV, but they read "Christian" books and watch "Christian" TV and listen to "Christian" pop; these folks are more likely to be found in the conservative evangelical, Pentecostal, or fundamentalist sector of the church. So what happens when you take someone from Group A and expose her to twenty-four hours of Group B in the form of an entire day and night of Trinity Broadcasting Network? That is the question Seabury Press asked me in the summer of 2007. A year later, this book is one answer to that question.

Honestly, my first reaction to the pitch from Seabury to watch twenty-four consecutive hours of TBN was "doesn't the Geneva convention address that somewhere, like right after waterboarding?" But soon the idea grew on me, and I began to think of it like Theological Fear Factor or Religious Super Size Me, which made it sound kind of fun. So my first question was, naturally, "Can I invite my friends?"

A whole slew of other questions soon followed. Previous to the writing of this book the whole of my exposure to TBN was limited to hotel room channel surfing accompanied by an exclamation like "What in the world?"

What little I knew about the world of Christian television I, to be honest, felt superior to. I also knew that while my first reaction to, well, almost everything, is sarcasm, the only thing that would make this project (or test of endurance, take your pick) interesting is if there were moments when I could move beyond snark and ask relevant questions of my subjects and myself. The questions gathering in my head as I prepared for my immersion experience began to take on a bit of an anthropological quality.

Actually, maybe pretending to be a professional would be the best approach. So what questions would famous primatologist Louis Leaky be asking? He'd be interested in mating, grooming, social structures, tool use, and food acquisition. Primatology is still the study of humans; we *are* primates after all. So in the end, what did I learn about myself as a Christian?

So in terms of mating and grooming: What messages about gender and beauty are given through the way in which the personalities are groomed and who gets to do and say what? Is there gender stratification? If so, what does it look like and can certain beliefs be extrapolated from this? Is sexuality addressed at all?

Social structures: What messages do I hear being proclaimed about wealth? Is there a discernible way in which class is being addressed? What is the connection between faith and wealth?

Tool use: How is the Bible used? Is there a consistent hermeneutic (interpretive lens) involved, or just simple prooftexting (using individual random Bible verses to back up your claim)? Even after years of theological training, did I learn something new? In what ways did the use or misuse of the biblical text make me wish to cause myself physical harm rather than keep watching. At any point did I find myself actually leaving my body, peacefully floating above the room watching myself watch TBN?

Food acquisition: Advertising. Who advertises? Is there continuity between the message of the advertisers and the message of TBN? In what ways does TBN encourage or discourage American consumer culture?

My own answers to some of these questions are found in the following pages, but others remained unanswered. Coming up with sarcastic remarks in response to the poor grammar (Creflo Dollar asking us to "stop living in unforgiveness") and questionable theology (someone on *PTL* praying to "Our heavenly father Jesus Christ") or both (Joel Osteen claiming that "God pleasures in prospering you") was of course, effortless. Significantly less comfortable were the moments when that window into TBN became a mirror.

I began to wonder what the TBN folks would think of me, a heavily tattooed Christian progressive from a liturgical denomination. How would people in their theological camp respond to *my* preaching? Would they think, as I do of them, that I misuse scripture? Would they be offended at the aesthetic in the community I serve? Would they dismiss my years of theological education as silly and unnecessary? When it comes right down to it, so many of my criticisms of TBN could go both ways, and if that's true then could it also be true, despite us both, that God is at work in my community *and* in (gulp) TBN? Let me just say, this is the last thing I want to be true because I love — seriously, I adore — being right. If I were Julie Andrews, I would be sitting around with a bunch of similarly dressed children singing a song about "raindrops on roses and me being right, other people being wrong and warm woolen mittens, brown paper packages tied up with string, these are a few of my favorite things." You get the idea.

Allowing for the possibility that God may be at work in both my community *and* TBN is not the same as conceding that TBN's theology and methods are sound. When I realized this, it disturbed me, but I haven't been able to shake the idea. I wrote once in a prayer, "Dear God, your work in the world is always done by sinners, or else it would never get done; help us to realize this and practice the grace and forgiveness you first gave us." But when I was talking about sinners in that case, it was just the broken beautiful people like myself and the others in my community, not my theological "other." Rather than fortifying my theological and ecclesiastical entrenchment, the experience of writing this book has strangely done the opposite. While maintaining that the prosperity gospel, the rapture, and Christian Zionism (all TBN fare) are up there with the selling of indulgences and the existence of purgatory as the stinkiest Christian ideas in history, I still must admit that God's redeeming work in the world does not happen only when we get all the theology and method right. As much as I hate to admit it, our theology, even when it's "good" theology (like mine, seriously it's *so* good; just ask me) does not save me from myself. One of the unexpected results of this project for me personally is that, surprisingly enough, I have developed a new friendship with an evangelical pastor. If you told me a year ago that this would happen, I'd say it would only be a sign of the end times, but there you go. We do not see eye to eye theologically, and likely we never will, but that's not the point. What my friend and I get by being in a relationship is an exposure to that which we do not get from our own traditions, and there is a lot missing on both ends. Sometimes the body of Christ is so busy trying to pretend that our particular form of Christianity is the most faithful, or the most biblical, or the most liberating (I include myself here) that we don't bother taking advantage of each other's traditions to help fill the inevitable holes in our own.

♦♦♦

Now might be a good time to explain something. I did this whole thing twice, not by choice but by necessity. On a Friday–Saturday last August I sat in my living room with about twenty-five of my friends (not all at once) and watched twenty-four hours of TBN (all at once) for this book. During the twenty-four hours I recorded the conversations onto my laptop and the twenty-four hours of TBN programming onto a digital video recorder in my cable box. (We actually had to *get* cable so I could do this project). Nine days later the hard drive on my DVR died. As in gone. Poof. Nothing. If you had come by my house that day you would likely have found me on the floor of my bedroom crying like a spanked child. After Kübler-Rossing my way through the stages of grief, denying the recording was gone, magically thinking maybe it had been erased due to a buildup of unconfessed sin on my part, and pleading with the cable company, my sweet editor suggested maybe I should just do it again. Some of my viewing friends from round one couldn't do round two, but some new folks could. The new date: November 2, 2007. I would have loved to schedule it sooner, but at the time I was commuting from St. Paul, Minnesota, to my home in Denver and my options were limited.

Putting together the guest list proved easier than I anticipated; all of the guests from round one whose schedules allowed agreed to come back, God bless 'em. I filled in the time slots with as random a mix of people as I could muster: Bible scholars, Lutheran pastors, a couple of Jews, a gay Episcopal priest, a lesbian Unitarian, a stand-up comic turned Methodist minister, my non-Christian ex-boyfriend, my evangelical parents, my old preaching professor, my eight-year-old daughter, and three people I had never met until they came to my house to watch some televangelism. Twenty-nine people in all. These are simply people in my life and do not even vaguely represent America, Christianity in general, the TBN audience, the Denver populace, or any other desirable cross-section. They are just my friends (well, except those three I'd never met before, but they're friends now).

♦♦♦

The night before I try to think of all the details. I stock the house with snacks and beer, set up the DVR to record for twenty-four hours, talk my parents into providing a back-up recording, set my alarm, set up my computer and microphone, place the guest list next to the computer, recheck that I set my alarm, and then pray. Now all I need is a decent night's sleep.

The Stranger
(*Seriously, my Savior would not wear bangs*)
5:00 a.m.

In defeat I turn off the alarm, which has been rendered useless due to the fact that I am already awake and tragically have been for the past two and a half hours. I awoke at 2:00 a.m. thinking, "If you don't go back to sleep you're screwed tomorrow," which produced just enough adrenaline to keep me awake.

Trying not to wake my husband, Matthew, I get out of bed to face the twenty-four straight hours of Trinity Broadcasting Network. Again.

So here I am, and there just isn't enough coffee in the whole world. My friends Jay and Annie, who'll be watching the 5:30 a.m. show with me, are asleep in the guest room downstairs, but I've decided I need to start this day on my own.

Coffee. Shower. Coffee. Pray. Coffee. Turn on the TV.

◆◆◆

Mysterious, who could this Stranger be? I wonder.

This show appears to be a made-for-TBN drama. We open on an African American diner. Chaos is swirling around this busy breakfast joint with the requisite cranky floor manager and flirty waitress. In walks a white man with an insidious smile and long, chlorine-damaged blond hair with, and I couldn't make this up, bangs. Is it really possible that a guy who looks like a creepy middle-aged yoga teacher from Boulder, Colorado, could be the second person of the Trinity? Well, maybe Jesus *would* wear a white V-neck sweater.

The flirty waitress (Mary) sits down with the Stranger, who is on his third or fourth cup of coffee (so he's clearly not the Mormon Jesus) and tells him how the diner used to belong to their dad before he died, but now she and her sister, the cranky floor manager, are left to run the place. She's distressed about the fact that unlike their dad, her sister opens the diner on Sunday to get the church crowd. She tells the Stranger that while she never misses church and she prays a lot, she has a lot of questions. "I wish Jesus would just come down and answer a few questions for me."

The Stranger: "Really? What would you ask him?" The camera pans down to a closeup of his crucifixion-scarred wrists.

"I'd ask him why Daddy had to die so suddenly and why Martha's fiancé moved away and never came back, and why I had to quit school and sling

9

hash for two-dollar tips." I'd have to add something about why *Growing Pains* lasted seven full seasons on ABC, but that's just me.

The Stranger: "No discipline seems pleasant, but painful. . . . But later it produces a harvest of righteousness and peace for those who have been trained by it." It's hard to believe that Jesus would go the "redemptive suffering" route. Didn't he go through that so we wouldn't have to? Still, the most difficult disbelief to suspend is that my Lord and savior would have bangs.

Their conversation is interrupted by Martha — "Excuse me," sarcastically to Mary. "Are we closed now? Those lunch menus aren't going to put themselves out." Oh my gosh. I get it now, *Martha and Mary*. Just like the gospel narratives about Mary and Martha, the sisters of Lazarus. This family was close friends of Jesus, and the story goes that one day Mary was hanging out with the guys listening to Jesus when her sister, Martha, started to passive aggressively slam dishes around in the kitchen to show how hard she was working in comparison to her slacker sister. When the passive thing didn't work, she implored Jesus to rebuke Mary for not helping out more. He, of course, told Martha to chill out. So this is a modern retelling of that story. I actually like the idea and, I almost hate to say it, other than creepy-Jesus, it's not too bad.

Mary sits in Jesus' booth again and after telling him charming childhood stories about how her daddy never turned away homeless folks from the diner but gave each one a sandwich and a cup of coffee, she confesses that Martha isn't quite so generous. Martha predictably interrupts their conversation to task Mary with filling the salt shakers. Next we see Jesus with a box of kosher salt, refilling shakers with Mary. If anyone pokes their head out of the kitchen and says, "We need to buy new yeast," I may have to leave the room for a few minutes.

Martha interrupts again basically to try to kick Jesus out for just hanging around. (I tried that in my twenties, and it just didn't work). The drama comes to a peak when Mary scolds Martha right back for opening on Sunday.

"Daddy wouldn't be proud of what you've done with the café. He'd be ashamed of who you've become." Ouch.

They both turn to Jesus to ask which one of them is in the right: Mary who wants to just kick back and enjoy life, or Martha the miserable workaholic. To which he says, "Both. In God's eyes it makes no more sense to spend all your time smelling the roses than it does to work yourself to exhaustion. . . . Enjoying God's love means balance."

To which Martha replies: "That sounds like something on *Oprah*. You can't just expect to live your life 50 percent one way and 50 percent the other." I have to say I'm with Martha on this one. I am fairly convinced that the whole "live a balanced life" thing is just another device society uses to try to make me feel bad about myself, much like commercials for Crest White Strips.

"Do you remember the broken-down playground across the street when you were kids?" Jesus, um, I mean the Stranger, asks the sisters.

"How do you know about that?"

"Remember what your dad would do to make the seesaw more fun? How he'd stand in the middle to keep it balanced"?

The sisters pause and say, "Keep our eyes on him." And I'm going to puke. The sisters turn around at the sound of breaking dishes in the kitchen. When they turn again, Jesus is gone. Only his empty coffee mug, five dollars, and a photo of them as young girls is left, which is a little Twilight Zone-ish. I'm just glad Jesus is a good tipper, though that in no way makes up for the bangs.

Final shot: a patron walks up to the diner, but the door is locked. The sign on the door reads, "Closed Sundays."

THE ROUNDUP

Thought for this show: Keep your eyes on God and your life will be balanced, but your teeth will be no whiter.

Paula White Today
(*Boosting God's self-esteem*)
5:30 a.m.

My guest Jay McDivitt is a Lutheran pastor in Denver, Colorado. After years of bouncing around Methodist, Lutheran, Episcopal, UCC, and Unitarian-Universalist communities, he now finds himself as a proud Lutheran, somewhere between a generous orthodoxy and a boundaried progressivism. He also loves to play poker, cook with garlic, and drink cheap wine with his lovely spouse.

♦♦♦

My guest Ann E. Williams grew up in Wisconsin, where she spent every Sunday in the Presbyterian Church USA. Her undergraduate experience at Luther College in Decorah, Iowa, converted her to the ELCA and a deep love of liturgy. A graduate of the Lutheran School of Theology in Chicago, Ann now spends her time as the ecumenical minister at a Jesuit university and also enjoys studying narrative theories of counseling.

(All guest biographies were written by the guest in question.)
◆◆◆

Much to my delight, Paula White is next. The last time I watched her show, her talk was entitled, "Why God Wants You Wealthy." White is a mega-church "pastor" along with her (soon to be second ex-) husband "Bishop" Randy White.

After years of seminary, I find myself getting a tad indignant about people taking the title "pastor" much less "bishop" with all the consideration and credentialing one might use choosing a chat room screen name.

With the litany of multi-million-dollar corporate jets and mansions owned by the likes of White and Creflo Dollar, the Crouches (TBN founders), and many other prosperity preachers, I'm beginning to become convinced that the income earned by preachers on TBN is inversely proportional to the amount of theological education completed. Perhaps something in the range of the following: for every year of college and graduate education earned past an associate's degree from a correspondence course one can expect to earn from $10,000 to $50,000 less a year.

My good friends Jay and Annie have groggily emerged from the basement. Between the three of us we have twelve years of postgraduate theological training and the combined yearly income of far less than $100,000 (not quite proving my point, but coming pretty close to it). I love these two for many things, not the least of which is the fact that they agreed to watch TBN at 5:30 a.m. and that after a particularly late clergy poker game last night.

Paula Today is nothing more than Paula White talking into the camera, and let me tell you, this girl can talk. She's a gifted orator, speaking into the camera in such a relaxed, charming, confident manner that I find myself unable to look away. She's absolutely mesmerizing — perfectly styled dyed-blond hair, fake French manicured nails, capped teeth, and enough botox in her face to taint the food supply of a small farm town. She's what fancy French postmodernist Baudrillard would call a *simulacrum* of a woman (an imitation for which there is no actual original). She's excited this morning to be bringing us a message on an "attitude of gratitude." As she talks I realize that she gestures not with her hands so much as with her fingernails. It's as if with every movement she is underscoring not only the meaning of her words but also the supremacy of her manicure.

Here's her argument:

1. I desire God's presence (Psalm 27).

2. God sets up clearly how to approach him (Psalm 100:5).

3. We must "do it God's way."

This "order" that she claims God has given us to enter into God's presence is that we must give a "thanks offering, an offering for fellowship or communion with God." The "thanks offering" thing is added onto the text in the Amplified Bible, which is, much like the name implies, a version of the Bible where the translators decided to add a little "umph," and so, like the Ted Turners of biblical publishing, have "colorized" the classic. So the psalm she's using says, "Enter his gates with thanksgiving and his courts with praise," but Paula then takes the "thank offering" addition of the Amplified version, and she runs with it — all the way to the bank.

◆◆◆

Paula offers this thought, "When you worship you are prostrating yourself before God, and you are submitting your sense of superiority to God." This is interesting to me. I have to give it to the evangelicals here; they seem to focus on worshiping God more than the dry liturgical types I run with. We tend to mistakenly conflate worship and liturgical precision, as though worshiping God is possible only when all the magical elements of confession, absolution, creed, Lord's Prayer, and the words of institution are done correctly and in the appropriate order. What *is* our doctrine of worship really?

Back to Paula: She's claiming that to be satisfied, fulfilled, peaceful, and joyful, "You have to do it God's way. God never asks that you understand him, just that you obey him." And this is going to be where White begins to make me crazy. I'm wondering: How do we determine what "God asks" of us? One biblical account says that all that God requires is to do justice, love mercy, and walk humbly with God. What does it mean to "obey" God? Are we, like the Hebrew people, to abide by the law of Moses and the Deuteronomic code? Really, Paula? I'm going to assume for the sake of argument that Paula would say that following the "rules" in the Bible is the same thing as obeying God. The problem with that line of reasoning is that the Bible is a huge book (really more like a library than a single book), and there are hundreds of rules or guidelines. Some rules we think of as God's will and others we ignore.

This is admittedly an easy target, but here are a few ways in which I am certain that Paula does not "obey God":

- Her outfit is made of more than one fabric (Lev. 19:19).

- She clearly cuts her hair (Lev. 19:27).

- While I can't prove this one, it's still worth mentioning on the merit of sheer weirdness: When (perhaps *if*) Paula goes camping, I hope that she designates a place outside of camp and then takes a small trowel with which she digs a hole to cover up her own shit, for this is to "obey God" (Deut. 23:12).

Yes indeed, two can play at this game, my prooftexting sister.

She quickly goes on to add that "if you want God's results, God says, 'This is the way you approach me,' this is the portal into my gates, first by a thanksgiving offering, to say, 'God I value you and this sacrifice is validation of your worthiness.'"

"Wow," Jay offers, "God is so needy. I've had girlfriends like that."

This idea of God is that God is a wealthy king with low self-esteem who arbitrarily makes up rules that have to be followed in order for his impoverished subjects to get anything out of him. Most of these rules involve the subjects acting sycophantically in order to boost God's self-worth. Oh, and this particular "rule" is found in one line of a psalm, so thank goodness we have the scholarly work of Paula White to help uncover this little mystery for us.

All of a sudden I realize that it's way too early in the morning to be feeling quite so cynical, and what if I use my cynicism all up and by hour ten or eleven then find myself agreeing with stuff that would normally make me want to convert to something less crazy, like, say, Branch Davidianism. I must pace myself.

◆◆◆

My efforts to back off the criticism are thwarted by Paula's next effort to back up her preaching. Paula uses a very effective tool for pastors and does a word study on "worship." Digging into the Greek text to look for what we might be missing in the English translation — because, despite what we'd like to think, translation is always interpretation — can really enlighten our understanding of the text. Paula, however, does a word study on the *English* word "worship." Jay and Annie have the funniest looks of disbelief on their faces. All three of us had to pass graduate-level Greek in seminary so that we can do Greek word studies while preparing for sermons. And here Paula White, millionaire preacher — with all the authority in her voice you can possibly imagine — is doing a word study on the English translation of a Greek word. She has a slide that shows that the word "worship" comes from an old Anglo-Saxon compound word, *weorth* (meaning value or respect) and *skype* (meaning to shape or build something). So together they mean to build or shape worth, value, or respect.

Paula follows this with a little pastoral care story about folks who she has counseled over the years coming to her with their relationship woes, and her suggestion is that the way for these situations to be resolved is to pray that Johnny, or whoever, "fall in love with Jesus." Then he will value that which God values. Johnny won't violate you because when he falls in love with Jesus he will honor you. The logical extension of this argument is that if Johnny is "violating" you and you pray in faith that he falls in love with Jesus, and he does not fall in love with Jesus, then you did not have enough faith. Ergo, you are to blame for the continuing violation. I hold an entirely different belief: there is no magic formula for "activating" God in our lives. God is a God for us, so we don't have to do that for ourselves. Maybe this sense of dignity that comes from being a created and redeemed child of God is enough to get the hell out of the relationship if Johnny is unable to reflect that love for you.

What's so disturbing is that TV preachers can dispense these magic formulas for health and wealth, tell people this is "God's way," and yet never be interrupted by the raised hand of someone who says, "I do all of the things you're saying but I'm still depressed" — or poor, or not speaking to my sister, or feeling as though God has abandoned me. This medium allows Paula White and her fellows, to some extent, to ignore the real, lived, *complicated experience* of people.

The irony of Paula telling this story about counseling folks in problematic relationships while in the midst of a divorce from "Bishop" Randy White is not at all lost on us.

Paula: "We'll be right back and I'll teach you how to come into the presence of God."

That'll be awesome, but I think I'll need some more coffee.

Advertisement: Paula's "Life by Design" at the Manhattan Center in New York. Get your tickets now.

◆◆◆

Despite the fact that Paula already defined the English word "worship," she goes for round two. "The other part of the compound word *wearth* and *skype* is 'ship,' and it literally means that when we worship God we are literally becoming ships or vessels submersed in his infinite worth and value."

A few things here. One, I'm not sure the word "literally" means what she thinks it means because, Paula honey, no matter how much Pentecostal you sprinkled on your breakfast cereal this morning, I'm still sure you don't really believe we *literally* turn into seafaring vessels. Two, I can't resist the temptation to look up this compound word in the online etymological dictionary. "Ship" is actually "the state or condition of being" and has nothing nautical about its origin. It is a synonym of *skype* and is not "another part of the compound word."

Her point, I believe, is that "darkness cannot exist in light" and that when we worship, the things that are dark scatter like cockroaches when we flip on the light of worship.

◆◆◆

Paula begins to tell a story of how she struggled with eating disorders. While playing a Bible trivia game as a "young believer," she fell on the kitchen floor worshiping God. (Paula, if you don't know the answer, just pass; you don't have to get all dramatic.) She claims that some of her bondage was lifted, but that she still had some left because "sanctification is a progressive process; you go from glory to glory to glory."

Matthew: "And by progressive, I don't think she means Jim Wallis."

I know that Paul in 2 Corinthians speaks about us reflecting the glory of God, which is beautiful but I think does not change the fact that we are sinners. What I have *no idea* about is what these people mean on a functional level when they say we go "from glory to glory to glory." I think I need an English-to-Evangelical dictionary. But I *do* know how I feel about progressive sanctification, namely, that it's hooey. And here's why: I believe, and my Lutheran tradition teaches, that we are all (watch me get all fancy on the Latin here) *simul iustus et peccator* — simultaneously saint and sinner. Back to my own sinfulness, which at this moment is taking the form of pointing out how bizarre our little Paula White is.

How does Paula wrap this message of how to come into the presence of God? By saying this: "Won't you have an attitude of gratitude and open up the spiritual possibilities by coming into the presence of God through entering in his gates with thanksgiving with a thanks offering, a peace offering, which says, 'God I'm bringing a sacrifice, I bring something of value to me [screen has an address and phone number with "honor God with a special thanksgiving offering"] in exchange for what is truly valuable... your presence.' Get up and call that toll free number right now or go to the website or PO box, but you have to do it God's way, enter his gates, his passage to the secret place of bringing God's presence into your life. Worship him with an offering saying thank you for what you have done when you call the toll free number and you sow your seed of sacrifice this thanksgiving season with an attitude of gratitude. I believe God has great things for you."

I just watched what could only be described as a preach-a-mercial. It's so similar to the feeling I get when I'm flipping through cable channels and see what seems innocently enough like a talk show or an exercise program, only to feel the sting of betrayal as the 1-800 number hits the screen. What bothers me the most is this: her insistence that "you have to do it God's way." That's a very insidious thing to say because the implication is that Paula White has some way of knowing what "God's way" is and that her teaching *equals* "God's way." Therefore not to follow what Paula says is equal to disobeying God.

I am also disturbed by the fact that we mainline progressive Protestants need to have a deeper focus on what worship means. Not that we have to adopt Paula's idea that worship is when we tell God how great God is while we're the middle of God's own furnace, like some "this hurts me more than it hurts you," or "it's for your own good" abusive logic. And worship certainly doesn't have to mean listening to "Jesus Is My Boyfriend" praise music in you car. But how can our vocations as the baptized be lived out in the world as a conscious act of worship? For doxological living is in the reality of us being fully creature and God Creator. God is then not something we tack on to our lives but is the source of life itself in whom we move and live and have our being.

THE ROUNDUP

Old Testament passages cited: Nine.

New Testament passages cited: Eight.

Cost of products offered: Depends on how much you want to get out of God's furnace.

Doctrine of God: God has low self-esteem and puts us in furnaces until we start to tell him how great he is; then he'll let us out.

Mentions of Jesus: One — Jesus' blood allows us to repent.

Cups of coffee: Two.

Thought for the hour: What does living a life of worship look like? Perhaps actually acting and living as though God is the source of all life.

Intermission

REFLECTION ON THE BLANK SCREEN

Simul Iustus et Peccator

THE LATIN ABOVE means "simultaneously saint and sinner," and, as a matter of fact, is tattooed around my right wrist (because, as I mentioned before, I'm just that much of a theological fancy-pants). Why, you may ask, get a fancy-pants Latin tattoo about sin on my wrist? Because in my tradition we hold that we are all 100 percent sinner and 100 percent saint. But wait, Nadia, you say, that's 200 percent. Well, yes and no. You see the two 100 percents are simultaneous. There is no process of sanctification, good works, prayer, yoga, recycling, Bible study, or holy living that makes us even 99 percent sinner and 101 percent saint. Much less like 10/190. As Luther says, we are at the same time the Old Eve (or Adam) and the New Creature. The really liberating thing about this is that when we all come to the table fully aware that we are sinners, that we are broken on some level and never perfect, then the temptation to pretend otherwise is greatly diminished. To embrace your sinfulness and saintliness is not the same as being intentionally immoral. It is to be realistic and to recognize that no one can possibly be 100 percent honest all the time, can always think of the neighbor before the self, can always honor God in everything we do, can at all times decrease in self so that others may increase. Even if our actions come close to this (they never do, but *if* they did) then we still are stuck with the reality of our minds and the thoughts of our hearts. When Jesus said in Matthew 5:28 that even if you *look* on a woman in lust you have committed adultery, this was not to set the bar so high that you feel defeated, or then again maybe it was exactly that. You see, the spiritual poison of our own righteousness is problematic (saying "here are the rules we must follow to please God and to be sanctified, and I follow those rules so I have good reason to be prideful about my sanctification because I earned it"). Jesus knew this was ridiculous. I like to think of him basically saying to those self-righteous guys, "If you seriously think you are without sin, you're just kind of an idiot." Of course that's the sarcastic Jesus in my head. Thank goodness the real Jesus is more gracious than I am.

Jesse Duplantis Ministries
(Being Charlie in God's chocolate factory)
6:00 a.m.

We all grab more coffee as Matthew, my husband, leaves to pick up the pastries I ordered from our local bakery. It's time for Jesse Duplantis, a very entertaining Cajun preacher straight from New Orleans. He looks a bit like Cornelius from *Planet of the Apes*, but in a silk suit and with a Cajun accent.

As we settle in I tell Jay and Annie about my favorite part of the only other Jesse Duplantis sermon I've heard, during which he talked about his "sinner friends." Here's an excerpt: "I believe you *should* have sinner friends. Jesus was a friend of sinners, but you should be stronger than the sin they are sinning."

Sinner friends? This of course begs the question: for whom is *he* the sinner friend? I like to think that if Jesse and I were buddies I'd introduce him as "Jesse, my sinner friend." I think I'm not unusual in saying that all my friends are sinner friends, because, other than my cat, they are all human.

It's hard for me not to assume that these TV preachers, when they talk about how they "once were sinners" really mean that they were once immoral and now that they are Christians they don't do the things Christians are not supposed to do and they do do the things that Christians are supposed to do.

♦♦♦

The teaser for today's show indicates that he's in the middle of a series entitled "Taking Ownership of What's Ours." And he starts at the Beginning. Literally. Jesse tells the creation story from his viewpoint, namely, that God existed and that the angels were created at the time God created the heavens, after which he created earth and sea and...oysters because "God knew a Cajun was gonna come and show people how to cook them. And he created trees with seeds already in them, so what came first the chicken or the egg?" Without the slightest hesitation or irony Jesse boldly proclaims, "The Chicken. Because without the chicken there is no egg."

Laughter explodes in my living room. We can't even breathe, except Jay, who manages to say "Could he now maybe unpack the whole 'why did the chicken cross the road' thing for us? That'd be awesome."

Jesse's trying to explain how jealous and angry the angels must have felt when God said, "Let us make man in our own image":

> The angels say "Man? What is that? You're going to make a new life species to look like you?" [God says] "Not only to look like me but for me to dwell in like a habitation." [The angels say,] "Why do you need them?" [God:] "Partnership." [Angels:] "But you have us." [God:] "I know, but I'm gonna give them something you don't have." Oh Lord, we're getting into some deep stuff here.

The audience is really worked up. Jesse goes on to claim that the reason Adam didn't take ownership of what was his is because he didn't understand himself. "But when I finish today, you're going to understand yourself." So God gives this species more power than any other species: dominion over the earth. "That's why Satan is jealous of you. You got something he didn't get."

"Wow, Satan's really petty, huh?" Annie adds. "So the devil hates us because we, like, have toasters and cell phones?"

"No," I respond, "that's why the Taliban hates us."

Jesse now refers back to the Genesis text: "Image and likeness of God. . . . whewww. What is man that thou visiteth him? I'm talking about taking ownership of what is ours. Because if you don't believe in yourself, you can't believe in anything. I learned that from Jesus. I always speak well of myself to myself." So at this point Jesse goes off a little bit about how he talks to himself in the mirror thusly:

> Do you know who you are? *Do* you know how much God loves you and will do anything for you if you ask in his name? Do you know just how good you are? Some think that is egotism. No. That's ownership. Didn't Jesus do that? He said, "I'm the way, I'm the truth, I'm the light."

I can't help but say "Um, but see, he was *Jesus*, and I'm thinking that's kind of what separates you."

Quoting a Stuart Smalley skit from *Saturday Night Live*, Annie says, "I'm good enough. . . . I'm smart enough. . . ."

Exactly.

Jesse continues, "I'm here to tell you who you are and what you own."

Annie: "There's a kernel of truth in this. . . . The Imago Dei is powerful."

I agree. As Lutherans with our whole simultaneously sinner and saint thing, I have to admit we can focus a little too much on the sinner and a little too little on the saint. We are, all of us, indeed the beloved of God. This idea of being a saint, of being the beloved, is so obviously dangerous when not paired with the reality that we are also sinners, but maybe the converse is also true. Not to live into the reality that we are children of God, the truly beloved, is perhaps just as harmful as thinking we are not still sinners.

♦♦♦

Jesse: "You're a totally different life species because he gave you ownership. Do you know anything [the angel] Gabriel owns? Have you read anywhere where [the angel] Michael owns something? They are in the army of the Lord, but God has given great things to man. We are the only species that he visits."

Annie interjects that "God doesn't visit Gabriel because they *live* together. He's probably sick of those guys anyway."

What, I wonder, are the great things God has given to man? Great things like the noble qualities one might have or the humanity that one might experience in God and in community, or are they great things like caramel corn and memory foam mattresses?

Jesse: "So man's function is to rule over all kingdoms of life beneath him."

Annie terms this, "The theology of manifest destiny."

Winding up the message, Jesse answers a big question and makes a bigger uh oh. "Why does man have dominion? Because he is a ruler. He is a king of kings and a lord . . . well, he's not the king of kings, Jesus is the king of kings but he's the king we king over." We all look at each other in disbelief. In the most profound Freudian slip while attempting to explain *who we are and what we own*, Jesse calls man the king of kings and lord of . . . oops. I think this is pretty telling. Trying to dig himself out from the "man is the king of kings" hole, he self-corrects by saying "Jesus is the king of kings," and then says "he's the king we king over." In all fairness, I'm not sure what he was *trying* to say. I only know what he *actually* said and it really wraps up his message nicely. We are the king of kings. God gave us all of the earth to rule over; it's all ours. We are the Charlie to God's chocolate factory; we just have to realize that we are Charlie and claim the candy.

The only problem is that ownership is not the same as caretaking. And this is an equally valid translation of that Genesis account. We are stewards, *not* owners. The earth and all that is in it belong not to us, but to God. We are charged with its care. And we're doing a bang-up job I must say. I wonder how much longer this "we can do anything we want to with the planet because God handed us the deed" line of thinking can continue. The good news here is that conservatives and liberals both theologically and politically have begun to come together over mutual concern for the care of the planet; Green Christianity is a growing movement, as well it should be. The only problem, of course, is with people like myself who are more likely to make "green" choices when they grant us a higher status in the new eco-tocracy, or are at least stylish, but crossing the line into genuine self-sacrifice? No thanks.

The show wraps up with Jesse in a studio talking directly to the camera about how Jesus gave us rulership over everything on the planet. "Get ready for something good; we just have to receive it in Jesus name."

What follows is an ad for *Voice of the Covenant* magazine, and a five-CD set, *Taking Ownership of What Is Yours,* for $59. Looking into the camera, Jesse is talking with the $59-CD set in his hands. "I'm telling you if you haven't ordered this yet you are missing God, because it is a great revelation from the Lord Jesus Christ." I'm thinking that would be a really effective thing to put on the back cover of the book. Forget endorsements from people who, unlike myself, are actual writers. We should just put in bold face, "If you haven't bought this book you are MISSING GOD! Because it is a great revelation from the Lord Jesus Christ." I'll be talking to my editor about that.

This is funny, but it is also seriously sad and scary and creepy. Jesse's story of the origin of earth and humans is not a biblical paraphrase of one of several creation accounts. This is an American, consumerist paraphrase that feeds directly into the darkest, shadow side of our culture — namely, salvation, identity, comfort, and security through *stuff.* This is the same as an infomercial that promises clear skin or tight abs or sharper knives, except it tugs on people's heartstrings and vulnerability and puts the powerful language of God and faith on a consumable good.

But wait! The pitch isn't over!

"I'm believing God for a million partners, so join this flagship of Jesse Duplantis ministries. We've got $1,000-a-month partners, we've got $10,000-a-month partners, and $10-a-month partners. Please call to be a part of this ministry. I promise you, we'll get somebody saved, I mean it, we'll get them healed too. This is Jesse saying [with a huge Cajun smile] I love you, bye bye."

I give over part of my Social Security check and it saves someone's soul?

◆◆◆

Ann: "Well, at least there's lots of diversity in these crowds."

Jay: "It's honestly a lot more diverse than most Lutheran churches. I'll give him that. And I'd love to have this guy over for a dinner party. He's hysterical."

Me: "You could be one of his *sinner* friends."

Matthew comes back from the bakery, "These pastries are hot."

Annie: "I'm going to take ownership over that scone right about now."

THE ROUNDUP

Old Testament passages cited: Twenty-eight.

New Testament passages cited: One.

Cost of products offered: $59 for CDs; $10, $1,000, or $10,000 a month to save souls.

Running total after 1½ hours: $179

Image of God: Willy Wonka-ish.

Mentions of Jesus: Two, using his name like a talisman and referring to the second person of the Trinity as a model of self-esteem.

Characterization of Satan: Insanely jealous that God gave human beings stuff and he got nothing to the point that, to this day Satan tries to pretend our stuff is really his. This is cosmic sibling rivalry at its worst.

Thought for the hour: What are mainline churches missing or not seeing that makes buying a CD from the likes of Jesse Duplantis more attractive than being in an actual community of faith?

Enjoying Everyday Life with Joyce Meyer
(*Am I a victorious, powerful,*
stomp-on-the-devil's-head Christian?)
6:30 a.m.

My guest Ann Graham Brock (Ph.D., Harvard University) is associate professor of New Testament at Iliff School of Theology and has written or edited numerous articles and books, including *Mary Magdalene, the First Apostle: The Struggle for Authority.* She received an Excellence in Teaching Award at Harvard University, and her television appearances include the History Channel, the Discovery Channel, and several British documentaries. Before getting her doctorate, she received her master's degree from Trinity Lutheran Seminary and continues to be active in the ELCA today.

◆◆◆

Jay and Annie are done with their shift but are staying past their allotted hour. I totally understand this because in some ways TBN is mesmerizing — kind of like *America's Funniest Home Videos;* you know it's bad, but if it's on you can't *not* watch it.

Dr. Ann Brock has joined us. Once or twice while I was taking Ann's New Testament class at Iliff School of Theology, she quoted something funny Joyce Meyer had said. I respect Ann quite a bit and know that she sometimes likes Joyce's frankness and sense of humor in her preaching, so I have invited her to join me for the hour. Ann appreciates that Joyce pokes fun and laughs at herself. Apparently Joyce was raised in a very conservative Christian tradition where women were forbidden to have any authority in the church, much less be preachers. Ann tells me that Joyce "felt a calling to preach, so she had to leave her church where she couldn't live out that calling, and in the process she lost everything, all of her friends and her community. It's a powerful story." I agree.

Joyce's show is called *Enjoying Everyday Life,* and the intro is a montage of people doing just that — laughing, having pillow fights, playing in a pile of leaves. But I have to tell you it's hard to see Joyce doing any of these things herself. She's now standing on a huge stage behind a large pulpit. She's dressed in slimming all black with a small gold sweater and dangly earrings. The audience numbers in the tens of thousands and appears to be mostly women.

She opens with a sternly voiced directive: "Open your Bibles up to 1 Peter, chapter 5, verse 8." She proceeds to read the passage (not surprisingly) from the Ted Turner colorized (Amplified, engorged, made-up, enhanced) version, and this does not go unnoticed by the New Testament scholar in the room, Ann comments, "It's weird that they always use the Amplified Bible."

"Dealing with the devil," Joyce announces, "is something we have to deal with all the time, so we might as well learn to do it right." She's talking about how thirty years ago as a good church member she didn't know what it meant that she was constantly struggling with someone who "wanted to steal my righteousness, peace, and joy and the good plan God had for my life."

She tells us that the devil roams around looking for open doors to mess with people. "God spoke to my heart a number of years ago." She claims, "He said, 'You can forget about open doors; the devil is looking for every tiny crack he can crawl through.' The more God blesses you, the more responsibility he gives you, and the more of God's anointing power and authority that's released in your life, the narrower your path must become. You may get by with things one year that you can't get by with the next year."

I hate to admit this, but I think she's right. The whole devil thing is weird to me, and I'll get to that, but I have to say that the closer I get to ordination, the more I struggle with things that haven't been an issue for me for years. My friend Kyle would put a Jungian twist on this and say that my shadow side doesn't go away just because I go to seminary. It's just that now I have no choice but to deal with it.

"As a believer in Jesus Christ, you have power and you have authority." Joyce has this strange mannerism where whenever she moves from the pulpit she clasps one hand over the other in front of her like an evangelical opera diva and stays like that while walking around the stage. It feels a bit like she's trying to control herself through a gesture management program.

"Turn your Bibles to Luke 10:19."

"Behold I have given you authority and power." (She reads from Luke 10.)

Joyce turns to the audience and says, "Say authority and power."

They comply.

"Don't you like those words? Say, 'I have authority.' [They do.] Say, 'I have power.' Say it again. 'I have authority.' 'I have power.'"

The camera pans to the audience of mostly middle-aged women saying, "I have power." I'm thinking about how empowering this must be to have one of their own speaking with such authority and telling them that they too have power. I'm thinking too of how ridiculous it would seem to me if I were there. I wonder then about my own criticism of these preachers. They all seem to be preaching to the disempowered, and I'm not really their target audience. Maybe these sermons that seem like self-help sprinkled with a few Bible verses, basically Oprah meets Jesus, really do help the powerless feel emboldened to claim some sort of control in their lives. How right is it for an empowered person to criticize the message? Well, in fairness, if Paula and Jesse and Joyce and Creflo were living comfortably middle-class lives like actual clergy folks, it would be harder still to criticize. But the fact of the matter is that their multi-million-dollar lifestyles are funded by the Social Security checks and low wages of their "ministry partners."

Joyce goes into a little thing on obedience. This is language that I can't stand, partly because I have huge authority issues and partly because I think "obedience" can be really abusive. I'm realizing that I'm not saying much of this out loud to Ann. I know she has a fondness for this woman, and I don't want to risk offending my former New Testament professor. Thankfully, I don't have to feel awkward for long because Ann soon volunteers her own criticism, "Sometimes this prooftexting can be bothersome." Ann adds, "I appreciate that she can be empowering and her humor can be really self-deprecating, but one of the difficulties I have is how she uses this empowerment language. She *is* a real leader with something to say, but then she can turn around and talk about her need to be submissive or obedient to her husband. She's an empowered woman who speaks the Word but then talks about being submissive to Dave. She doesn't talk about being equally yoked and partners, just the submissive stuff. There's this dichotomy that disturbs me. Maybe that's a throwback to her origins. Maybe she thinks she needs to be submissive so she doesn't lose her audience."

I find Ann's comment interesting, especially because Joyce hasn't really mentioned the whole "men having most-favored-gender-status in the eyes of the Almighty" issue at all. Yet Ann comments on it. Then I realize that Dr. Ann Brock, myself, and "Dr." Joyce Meyer are all in the same boat in a way. We all were raised in Christian traditions that did not allow women to "have authority over men." In my case this included forbidding women to usher or even help pass the collection plates. I never understood how handing a man a bulletin or collection plate was an exercise of authority, especially when we all knew that forty-five minutes later at the potluck I'd be handing that same man a plate of fried chicken. Handing him a plate in the "auditorium" ("sanctuary" was too Catholic sounding): no. Handing him a plate of Colonel Sanders: fine.

A list of things we must do in order to have a good relationship with God follows:

> Being a victorious, powerful, stomp-on-the-devil's-head Christian is
> a full-time job. One little sermon on Sunday morning is not going

to keep you in victory. You're going to have to love the word, live in the word, you're going to have to put time into your walk with God, you're going to need to study, you're going to need to pray, you're going to need to say no to things that keep you from having time with God. Remember the promises of God are for who-so-ever *will.*

My issue with this is that the ball is totally in our court. Maybe God is actually at work in the world and we can't see it, much less participate in it, when we are spending so much time trying to tend our relationship with God alone in our rooms reading our Bibles. Don't get me wrong. I love the biblical text, and most mornings I actually manage to read the daily office readings. But silently reading the biblical text, much less any text, is a somewhat modern invention, although we think of it as a given. Spiritual discipline as a part of Christian life I have no problem with. It's (*a*) doing it so that we will get something back from God, and (*b*) locating the activity of God in the world solely in some sort of quiet personal interior relationship in the individual that I find problematic.

Joyce Meyer claims that the reason some people are closer to God than others is not because God plays favorites, but because some people are willing to put more time into the relationship than others. There's a decent crowd for her talk, but she scoldingly claims that there should never be empty seats at something like this, which to me seems to go beyond speaking as a "victorious" Christian and just a few inches into the realm of narcissism.

Going back to the devil, Joyce tells us that "the devil hates you. He wants you to be miserable and to be a Christian with a bumper sticker and no fruit in your life. Think of the mental image most people have of Christians." Head hanging she shuffles across the stage pathetically saying, "Just trying to make it through till Jesus comes back to get me, can't wait to get to heaven," and the crowd cheers as she straightens up and says strongly, "Well, Jesus isn't like that. He's the Mighty Warrior, the Captain of the Hosts." They go wild. I'm wondering which Jesus she's referring to?

She continues by talking about how we aren't supposed to resist our circumstances. We are supposed to resist acting like the devil within our circumstances. The goal of every Christian should be to always be stable despite circumstances, not simply happy when things are good and sad when things are bad — which sounds very Buddhist to me. "Paul prayed that they would endure hardship with good temper," Joyce says, "and I pray that over our ministry partners at least a few times a week." If we can resist reacting to our circumstances, according to Joyce, then we can be like Jesus, who took a nap in the boat during the storm. He wasn't bothered while everyone else was freaking out.

I see where she's coming from in terms of trying to trust God even when things are a bit dodgy in our lives, but this is not the same as needing to not be sad when things are bad or happy when things are good. Jesus wept at the tomb of Lazarus. He didn't placidly experience the grief and mourning around the death of a friend with emotionally disaffected distance.

Advertisement: $25 set that includes the book *Eight Ways to Keep the Devil under Your Feet* and the DVD *Be Aggressive and Be Bold.*

"Remember that we love you, and we want God's best for you," Joyce says to the folks at home, now from inside a small studio. Once again we see a TBN preacher tell the viewers that (1) God wants good things for you, and (2) "I love you." Which makes me wonder: How often do these people who watch daytime Christian TV hear these two statements? What disturbs me is that this so-called love between Joyce Meyer and her TV viewers is *not pastoral care.* You can become a ministry partner and give Joyce Meyer your entire measly pension and she's still not showing up with a casserole when your mother dies. She's not showing up ever.

What follows is a commercial for Joyce Meyer's books, CDs, and wall calendar for "those who need to be uplifted in the Word," along with a set of "uplifting" coffee mugs. The disturbing merchandising of the hour award has to go, though, to the *Everyday Life* Bible with Joyce Meyer's name in very large type at the bottom — Yes, that's right — of the Bible! (available in bonded leather or paperback). This is Joyce Meyer's Study Bible based on — wait for it — the Amplified Version! This "Bible" is so many generations removed from the Greek text that it's about as closely related to the biblical text as is the *Farmer's Almanac* or the latest issue of *Comso.*

The voiceover advertises these Joyce-Meyer-related products with the following claim: "Remember, when you purchase Joyce Meyer products you are helping to spread the gospel all over the world, and there's no greater gift you can give than to introduce someone to the son of God" — which sounds so very pre-Reformation to me. "When a coin in the coffer rings, another soul from Purgatory springs" was a phrase used to get the subliterate of the sixteenth century to give their money to the ones who, like Joyce Meyer, could tell them what the will of God is and how to save souls. Theologically preying on the desperate and earnest in order to line one's own pockets is nothing new.

Advertisement: Joyce Meyer's Conference Tour. "Joyce wants to focus on you. If you're ready to really experience God in your life, this is your time." Joyce says to the camera, "You're going to have a great time, and I can't wait to see you there. You mean more to us here at Joyce Meyer ministry than you may ever know. We appreciate you and thank our friends and partners for making this worldwide ministry possible."

◆◆◆

My kids just woke up and are now sitting in my lap while Mommy talks to her friends about the devil, which is a pretty interesting way to start the morning, I'm sure.

We all agree that this stuff with the devil makes our own sinfulness exterior to us. If all the problems in our life or temptations we face are projected onto Satan, an external force of evil which is trying to take away "our joy," then we don't have to face the fact that *we have seen the devil and it is us.* But I'm still not satisfied about the fact that we don't have a theology of Satan in our church. I'm not saying that we should adopt the "Satan is trying to mess with you" thing, but I don't think it's good to just set the entire issue aside. We have to deal with evil in its human and nonhuman sources. The devil is in our small catechism (Christ defeats sin, death, and the devil) but you'd be hard pressed to preach on it. In our post-Enlightenment world we can't deal with the anthropomorphizing of evil in the form of a devil. At least I can't see the devil as much more than a charming but naive character in a folk tale.

The problem right now is that I can't figure out the issue of evil because my kids have to get off to school and the next TBN show starts in about fifteen seconds. I'm pretty fired up. I'm one cup of coffee and another prosperity gospel preacher away from being a *victorious, powerful, stomp-on-the-devil's-head Christian.* Almost.

THE ROUNDUP

Old Testament passages cited: Zero.

New Testament passages cited: Three.

Cost of products offered: $225.

Running total after 2 hours: $404

Mentions of Jesus: Two, as a character in a story and named as a "Mighty Warrior."

Changing Your World with Dr. Creflo Dollar
(Resisting the cherry danish with God's help)
7:00 a.m.

"Dr." Creflo Dollar's *Changing Your World* opens with a montage of happy families and individuals (much like the opening sequences for all the other shows so far, but with more African Americans). The theme song is decidedly gospel: "I'm a world changer, anointed with the power of the Holy Ghost, I'm a world changer."

He's preaching to a mostly African American congregation numbering in the thousands. Dollar is a handsome African American man in his forties. The gray suit he's wearing is silk, and I'm betting it's custom. The stage is all decked in royal blue with purple carpeting. A large gospel choir, resplendent in blue robes, sits behind him.

◆◆◆

"Wow," Ann says when she sees the show title. "This guy is a doctor?"

"Only in the way that Benny Hinn, Joyce Meyer, Paula White, and Jesse Duplantis are doctors. They were all given honorary doctorates from Oral Roberts University."

Dr. Dollar: "We've been talking about why God allows trials in our lives. Is it because he's trying to be mean? Absolutely not. Is it because he himself is the destroyer? Absolutely not. But will God allow trials and temptations and tests and hard times to come in our lives? The answer is yes."

Doc Dollar offers four reasons for this:

1. He loves us and wants us to be healed, to be whole, and to have abundant life. God allows trials in our lives because he knows where our rebellion against his word and our hard-headedness is going to take us.

2. He's trying to get your attention. Which is the purpose of this sermon.

3. He wants every hindrance removed that keeps us from fully yielding ourselves to God.

4. He wants us to love him: "God will never allow a trial without giving us a way to escape it."

[My own: That's just how life is.]

If you have a temptation, test, or trial, the first thing you need to know is that you can resist it. You have the ability to resist. Say out loud, "I have" [the audience echoes "I have"] "the ability" ["the ability"] "to resist" ["to resist"] "temptations and trials" ["temptations and trials"]. You're not going to go through something someone else hasn't already gone through; it's not going to be beyond human experience.

I tell Ann Brock, "That's what got me through labor with both my kids. I thought to myself, 'Being in labor may feel like it's the craziest, most intense, unusual thing in the world, but actually it's pretty darn common. Billions of women have gone through this, so you can too.'"
Dollar:

"God is faithful to his word and to his compassionate nature, which means that God ain't never gonna get so mad that he ignores his compassionate nature, so no matter what trial you are going through God is faithful to his word and his compassionate nature."

This is a lovely sentiment, but it's not in 1 Corinthians 10:13. The whole Amplified Bible thing is making me just a little crazy. The text he is using from 1 Corinthians does not talk about God's compassionate nature. The writers of the Amplified Bible added that. That particular translation of the Bible was undertaken in the 1950s by the Lockman Foundation, which on its website says the following about the project:

The Amplified Bible is a translation that, by using synonyms and definitions, both explains and expands the meaning of words in the text by placing amplification in parentheses and brackets and after key words or phrases. This unique system of translation allows the reader to more completely grasp the meaning of the words as they were understood in the original languages. Through multiple expressions, fuller and more revealing appreciation is given to the divine message as the original text legitimately permits. The Amplified Bible is free of personal interpretation and is independent of denominational prejudice.

The doctrine of scripture that holds that God verbally inspired the writers of the texts and was present and active in the entire process of the Bible being created is not at all uncommon among TBN folks. This is fine, but when they preach not from the biblical text, but from the added bits in the Amplified Bible and then treat them as having as much authority as actual biblical texts, things get confusing for me. I wonder if they think the guys who added all that stuff in the 1950s were also guided by the Holy Spirit, as if the Holy Spirit just kind of took a long sabbatical until the 1950s and then came out of retirement just for that gig. I'm all for looking at different ways to translate Greek, but Dr. Jim Boyce, my revered New Testament professor at Luther Seminary, who has been teaching Greek since shortly after the original texts were written, reminded us that "all translation is interpretation." There's no way to get around that.

I can't think about this anymore because I'm missing some preaching and despite all this stuff I actually kinda like this guy. He's totally charming.

I'm impressed with the fact that his whole congregation has open Bibles in their laps and all seem to be busy taking notes. Lutherans don't really bring Bibles to church. I'm not sure why that is. The lectionary texts are printed in most Lutheran church bulletins, and so if they want to follow along they only have to flip over the announcements, and there are the four texts, one each from the Hebrew Bible, the Psalms, the epistles, and the gospels. One problem this creates is that then no one opens up his or her own Bible. And in some churches when the lectors get up to do the readings, they don't open up a huge lectern Bible; they just read off the bulletin insert. We seem less like a People of the Book and more like a People of the Bulletin Insert.

"If you are going through a trial or test," Creflo insists, "God has already guaranteed and promised that you can win. So win! Amen!"

In my fundamentalist Church of Christ upbringing, however, we brought our Bibles to church, boy howdy. As a matter of fact, if you were a particularly righteous woman, you would carry your Bible in a quaintly quilted Bible cover with a lacy handle — like Laura Ingalls Wilder. I remember my father's Bible being clothed in a zippered leather cover complete with an inlay of a sword on the front. When we'd be late for church and my dad couldn't find his Bible, he'd yell, "Has anyone seen my sword?" I'm sure calling a Bible a sword comes from a verse, but I can't remember which, but the whole sword thing is a bit too Knights Templar for my taste. My friend Seth, who always can outdo my crazy "growing up Christian" stories, claims that as a child her family would do "sword drills" where her dad would grasp a Bible by the spine and shout out a verse, like "Leviticus 15:16," and then the kids would race to grab the Bible and look up the verse as quickly as possible. Full contact competitive Bible looking-up game, yep, a little crazy.

Seth's coming at one o'clock in the morning for the Bible trivia game show slot. I don't stand a chance.

Dollar:

> There's nothing you're going to be facing that you're not going to have the ability to win over. "Well, brother Dollar, I used to be a drug addict, and somebody came up to me with some cocaine." You know what? God wouldn't have allowed him to come up to you with some cocaine if you did not have the ability to resist him [congregation: *Amen*]. "Well, but you don't understand now. I love me some women, and if a good-looking woman comes up." Well, you know you can resist her. She can shake till her girdle pops loose and it won't bother you a bit because you have the ability to resist. Somebody shout, "I have the ability to resist!" [I have the ability to resist!]

Me: "I have the ability to resist this cherry danish, but I am choosing not to."

◆◆◆

Suddenly there is simply not enough coffee in the entire world for what I'm trying to do here. Twenty-two and a half hours to go.

Advertisement: Taffi Dollar's book: *21 Days to Your Spiritual Makeover,* $19.99.

"Creflo Dollar ministries is dedicated to changing the lives of others," the announcer says. "To help us to continue to make a difference, consider making a financial gift and start changing the world one person at a time. It is people like you who make it possible to spread the word of God."

◆◆◆

Ann gives her own response: "I think he seems sincere and contextual. He has a word he speaks to his audience, a word of comfort and how to get through trials and temptations. That is a theological difference for us — where God is present in an almost manipulative way. I call it parking space theology."

Me: "Yeah, God involved or intrusive in a moment-to-moment way. The language is so different from what we are used to. But I think he speaks in ways that are meaningful to people, or he wouldn't draw such crowds. We Lutherans have such theological pride."

Ann laughs, "Yeah, that's kinda true."

I add, "It can make it really hard to hear theology that we think doesn't stand up. It makes me wonder, what would Creflo Dollar think of my preaching? If I was preaching in my context and he was watching in his living room, what would he say?"

THE ROUNDUP

Old Testament passages cited: Nineteen.

New Testament passages cited: One.

Cost of products offered: $19.99 for Taffi Dollar's book.

Running total after 2½ hours: $423.99

God: Much like a manipulative boyfriend or girlfriend who tests you to see how much you really love him or her.

Thought for the half-hour: Send Creflo Dollar my preaching tape. Ask for comments.

John Hagee Today
(At the Ethan Allen Middle East
Apocalyptic News Desk)
7:30 a.m.

My guest Rev. Michael Fick is pastor of Epiphany Lutheran Church in Denver, his first call out of seminary. He was raised in a conservative Lutheran church with little liturgy, so now he enjoys pastoring at a progressive Lutheran church seeking beautiful, meaningful liturgy.

He's interested in the future of the urban neighborhood congregation and ponders how to explore emerging models for worship and church in a multigenerational context.

◆◆◆

Michael is a good friend and regular member of our Lutheran clergy poker game (along with Jay and Annie of 5:30 a.m.–6:30 a.m. fame). He's so smart and funny that it hurts me a little bit every time we're together. This morning he's maybe just a bit too excited about signing up to watch what he calls "The 7:30–8:30 John Hagee/Rod Parsley sucker punch."

Turning to Ann Brock, Michael says, "I just love it when Hagee gets the big *Borders in Time* posters behind him and goes straight up John Nelson Darby dispensationalism. That's my favorite."

Dispensationalism: A certain reading of the Bible that looks for signs of the end times, especially concerning ages, eras, and borders in time. Darby is the guy who made up the rapture, which a whole lot of people think is actually found in the Bible. See Left Behind series for details.

Oh, this is going to be fun, which is good because I find the pro-Israel stuff on TBN to be tedious and boring. I know I should care, but when it comes to Middle Eastern politics, with its few millennia of backstory, countless characters, and plot twists, I feel that I'm as likely to understand what's going on as I am to get what's happening with *Lost* based solely on episode 16. I wish, I really do, that I could watch Hagee and know exactly where he's going wrong politically, but I'm ill equipped. He could say Elvis is the prime minister of Israel and I'd have to go with it. This is humiliating, but I felt it best to just put it out there.

From the international media center in San Antonio, Texas, a special presentation from John Hagee Ministries. Today Pastor John Hagee introduces his latest book, *In Defense of Israel.*

Music, desk, and chair all suggest "news program," as opposed to sermon. Hagee is using the half-hour to pitch his latest book, which he calls his "twenty-second major book — and it covers the waterfront when it comes to relationships between Christians and Jews." He's sitting on a set that screams both "nicely appointed" and "Ethan Allen": dark wood, books, and leather. It manages to be manly and fancy at the same time. Hagee is jowly and angry and looks, though I'm no medical expert, like he may possibly be bloated on his own hate.

He goes right into the apocalyptic Israel stuff. "God is going to raise up a body of Gentile people who are going to support the Jewish people." He claims that Israel is in great danger and that Iranian president Ahmadinejad wants Israel to be wiped off the map by a nuclear storm.

Fick: "Do you think folks on the right have all agreed to say nu-cu-ler as some sort of defiant act?"

Hagee: "Iran wants to come to America and attack us. If Iran gets nuclear weapons it will be disastrous for America. If America leaves Iraq then Iran will fill that void. Because of our dependence on foreign oil, Iran could destroy the U.S. economy. They will also have the wealth to buy nuclear weapons."

Fick: "I think it's really interesting. Are people self-conscious about getting their news from Hagee? I have an uncle who calls Bill O'Reilly 'the news.'"

Hagee:

The FBI says there are even major cities in America marked for these nuclear weapons. If we defend Israel we defend ourselves. With Russia's assistance, Iran has the ability to bring Western civilization to its knees. If we defend Israel, then God will bless us. The Bible makes it clear in Genesis 12:3, "I will bless those who bless you and curse those who curse you."

Oh, goodness. In just five minutes we've gotten the crippling of the U.S. economy, nuclear holocaust in Israel and the United States, and the end of Western civilization. Is this guy available for children's parties? He's more terrifying than a birthday clown.

I'm a little distressed by people who preface their point by saying, "The Bible is really clear." I defy anyone to read a single book in the Bible and say everything seemed "clear."

♦♦♦

Hagee uses several prooftexts to show that God curses those who curse the Jewish people and blesses those who bless the Jewish people. Hagee:

Zechariah 2:8: Jews are the apple of God's eye. Where are the Babylonians, the Romans, the Ottoman Empire, where are Adolf Hitler and his lunatics? They are dead and buried in the bone yard of history because they cursed the Jewish people.

Luke 7:1–5: The centurion wanted Jesus to come into his house. Jesus visited him because he had done something practical to bless the Jewish people so Jesus broke the laws of Moses to enter the Gentile house to heal the girl.

Acts 10: Cornelius was praying for the Jewish people. Peter saw a sheet of unclean animals and the sheet was a prayer shawl and the animals were the Gentile people. Why did the message come to their house first? They did something practical to bless the Jewish people.

Fick: "That's kinda cool. I've never heard of it as a prayer shawl. I always call it a tablecloth, and I think in my sermon a few months back I called it a "buffet of abominations." But did you notice that we've just gone from Zechariah to Luke to Exodus to Genesis in four sentences. He sits down and decides what the Bible says, and then looks for verses and half-verses to back him up"

Me: "I'm right and you know why? God agrees with me!"

Hagee:

Romans 15:27: If the gentiles have benefited from the Jewish spiritual things, then the Gentiles owe it to the Jewish people to bless them with material things. What spiritual things have we received from the Jewish people? Every word of the Bible was written by Jewish hands. They gave us the patriarchs and the prophets; there's Mary, Joseph, and Jesus; the twelve disciples; and the apostle Paul. If you took away the Jewish contribution there would be no Christianity. It's time to stop praising the dead Jews of the past — Moses, Jacob, Abraham — while criticizing the Jews across the street from you, because that is anti-Semitism and anti-Semitism is a sin and as a sin it will damn your soul.

As a rule I'm not down with the whole hell and damnation thing, but I may have to agree with Hagee on making an exception for anti-Semitism.

Fick: "Hagee's pedigree is like, Baptist preacher begets Baptist preacher begets Baptist preacher, and I suspect his background had to be intensely anti-Semitic, so this may actually be a step in the right direction, although once Jesus comes back I think Hagee would say the Jews will either convert or be cast into the lake of fire, so it's not all good."

Me: "Yeah, I think joining hands and singing "We Are the World" might be a bit premature."

Hagee: "We have started Christians United for Israel so that every person in this nation who wants to support Israel can do so. This and much more is found in my book *In Defense of Israel.*"

◆◆◆

Cut to a John Hagee Ministries ad complete with images of Hagee laying hands on the heads of various folks as a voiceover tells us: "Miracles happen every day for those who know how to release the healing power of God. Pastor Hagee wants you to meet God's conditions for a miracle and he has prepared a special healing package."

Advertisement: Book and CD ($25).

Off the top of my head I can think of the following conditions for healing in the New Testament: You have faith (the woman with hemorrhages who touched Jesus' garment, Matt. 9, Luke 8, Mark 5). You may or may not have faith, but your friends do (the guy who was lowered through the ceiling, Mark 2). You not only have no faith, but you don't even know the name of Jesus (the lame man at the Bethesda pool who, when asked who healed him, said, "I don't know, some guy," John 5). Actually now that I think about it, the only condition for healing is that you are sick. That pretty much covers everyone, so I'm wondering why it is that Hagee thinks he has uncovered some sort of secret.

Advertisement: Israel: The Apple of God's Eye, CD for $13 or DVD for $25.

◆◆◆

I have decided to call the prayer line. Am not sure what I'll say.

Prayer line busy. Back to Hagee at the Ethan Allen Middle East Apocalyptic News Desk.

Fick: "As critical as I am of our own tradition, I have to say that I like our very low anxiety about the end times. When Luther was asked what he would do if he knew Jesus was coming back tomorrow, he said 'I'd plant a tree.'" That might be apocryphal Luther, but I'm with Fick on that one.

Prayer line still busy.

◆◆◆

Finally, the hour ends with an ad for *Against All Odds,* a TV movie about miracles of the Israeli army ($27), and one for a Fabergé-style egg, complete with "jewel-like" emblems and containing the holy family. Everything about the egg screams TBN, and it can be yours for a love offering of $250.

◆◆◆

Well, even if a nuclear holocaust and the end of Western civilization are imminent, it's 8:00 a.m. and the need of my children to get to school is even more imminent, so I take a ten-minute break.

THE ROUNDUP

Old Testament passages cited: Nine, plus the Book of Esther and a few chapters in Genesis.

New Testament passages cited: Ten.

Cost of products offered: $340

Running total after 3 hours: $763.99

God: Sovereign, and with some pretty specific requirements of us that, if unfulfilled, will cause God to not protect us against the terrorists and thus bring down all of Western civilization and the Muslim extremists will win.

Jesus: He was a nice guy when he was here the first time, but will be a bad ass the next time. Watch out.

Thought for the half-hour: If God smites us for not supporting the state of Israel, then the terrorists win.

Breakthrough with Rod Parsley
(*Do the prayer line people*
have to use stripper names?)
8:00 a.m.

Rod Parsley sits behind a leather-top desk amid an office full of ferns, the warmth of both his private study and his man tan allowing him to appear leisurely authoritative.

Parsley opens with a thank-you to his "partners in ministry," who fund his ministry. His voice is undeniably "Southern TV preacher," but it sounds so deeply affected that it's like he's actually making fun of himself.

At the bottom of the screen an ad flashes for Parsley's book *Culturally Incorrect* ($15).

◆◆◆

"Nothing will change for you, " Rod says, " until the pain of your present . . . now I'm talkin' to somebo-day. The pain of your present is greater than the fear of your future."

What does he mean "I'm talking to somebody"? It's as though he is trying to imply that there is a specific person watching for whom his message is addressed. Could it be me?

I feel the prompting right now from the Holy Spirit to pray for someone watching at this moment.

It is me! Weird.

I believe there is a stranglehold on your life and no matter what it is you can't seem to break free. Perhaps it's an addiction, maybe cigarettes or alcohol, I don't know. Maybe it's a seemingly insurmountable debt that has you in its clutches. . . .

[They cut to a closeup image of a someone sorting a stack of bills, and I think, "Wait a minute, how could they know he was going to have a prompting from the Holy Spirit?"]

Perhaps you've got a struggle in your family. I sense that very strongly. [Images of two people hugging.] Whatever is holding you back from fulfilling your assignment for God.

I'm a bit underwhelmed by Parsley's prophetic chops here. Cigarettes, debt, and family conflict? That's pretty boilerplate, isn't it? If Parsley said, "I sense that a heavily tattooed Lutheran woman who swears like a truck driver is struggling with the fact that she is lacking generosity in her assessment of my show today," I'd sign over my advance check for the book.

He's now praying for "his friend's struggle," while he's actually still hamming for the camera. (Note to self: praying in front of a camera with your eyes open is kind of creepy; never do this.)

I decide this is a good time to try the prayer line. I have a lot of questions about what exactly a "prayer line" is. A woman named Terry asks for my prayer request. I dodge the question with a few of my own.

Me: "Hi, Terry. I'm curious about your prayer line. Where are you guys and what's it like to work there?"

Realizing she's not likely to answer, I get nervous and just keep going. "Who calls in and what do they want? I was just curious about what a prayer line is."

Terry: "We don't give out any information. If you don't have a prayer request, I have to move on to the next caller."

Me (fumbling to recover): "I just wondered what it's like."

Terry: "Ma'am, do you have a prayer request?"

Me: "I guess not."

Terry: "Thank you." (Click.)

Darn. I wonder if I kept trying, would I eventually get a rogue prayer line employee who would gladly dish?

Parsley has now moved to pleading for help for the Christians in Sudan:

A radical Islamic fundamentalist regime has tried to enforce its misguided ideology on the Christian population of the southern half of Sudan. Thousands have been taken into captivity by Muslim slavemasters.

The plight of Christians in Sudan is of course quite real, but I am wondering about the whole prayer line thing again — curious if they pray with you on the phone or if they just promise to add you to the list. Do they ask for money after the prayer? I give it another try. Phone rings once, then a recorded voice thanks me for calling. "To donate money press 1. For a prayer press 2." I press 2 and am told that there is an approximately seven-minute wait time. I wonder if there would be a wait time if I pressed 1. I'll hold.

Parsley: "Let me remind you that these Sudanese exiles pray to the same Lord Jesus Christ for their daily bread that you call upon. They have the same hopes and desires as you, but most importantly they serve the same God. [He looks up when he says God.]"

Fick: "I love how he looks up when he talks about God."

Me: "Yeah, eye contact is *really* important to God."

Based on the first three verses of Psalm 41, Parsley claims that God offers a "sevenfold blessing" for you if you send money to Parsley to help the Sudanese Christians. God will:

1. deliver you in times of trouble

2. preserve you from contamination of the world

3. keep you alive

4. bless you on the earth

5. protect you from every enemy

6. strengthen you

7. raise you up if you have sickness in your body

He's promised to release his promises if you help his people in Sudan. He's given you a divine assignment to be their Moses.

◆◆◆

I almost forget I'm on hold until I hear the deep warm voice of an African American man on the line. His name is James, and I wonder for a second if that's his real name. Do they have to have fake ones like strippers? I tell him that I was hoping he could pray for me because I am writing a book. I decide not to disclose much more than that, which I feel kind of bad about. He asks me my name and I tell him "Lisa," which is actually not a lie. It's my first name, but I hate it so much that everyone in my life is under a gag order to not ever call me that, so it feels weird, in a different way, that I just told him to.

Father God, give Lisa [I cringe] the spiritual fortitude of a writer. I ask that Lord God, as she prepares the manuscripts that you would quicken her spirit and her mind to interpret all she has before her, so that when it comes on to the paper that it surprises even her. I ask that your guidance helps others in their reading. Give her the time to think and focus on what she is writing, and that with the anointing of God she might write with supernatural energy of the Holy Spirit.

Amen. I thank him, hang up, and realize that I didn't want him to stop. It was so beautiful. What I expected, I'm not sure, maybe a canned prayer of some sort leading to a plea for money, or maybe something more, I don't know, Pentecostal. But this was touching. I hadn't actually realized how much anxiety I had about this project until this stranger on the other end of the phone line asked God to guide me. I feel bad that I called thinking it would be more fodder for my mocking commentary. I'm not exactly sure what "writing with the supernatural power of the Holy Spirit" means, but if someone offered it to me, I'd not refuse it.

◆◆◆

Cut to Parsley in a different studio.

After more words about the plight of the Sudanese and an appeal for money, Parsley looks into the camera and says: "Until the next time please remember that I will be right here praying for the blessings of God to overtake you as you yourself become a deliverer to those in bondage."

◆◆◆

The little talk-to-the-folks-at-home personal message at the end of these shows is really disturbing, mostly because I'm sure it's effective. These people at home who watch Rod Parsley or Paula White or any of the TBN preachers, maybe they really do feel a personal connection to them. I guess my question is: What are we as the church not doing that creates this situation. Is a TV preacher telling you "I love you" the only human contact these folks are receiving? My friend John Backe, pastor at Our Savior's Lutheran Church in Denver, told me a story about when he was a new pastor at his first church right out of seminary. He resolved to visit all the "shut-ins" in his first month. One elderly brother and sister who he visited had TBN on the whole time he was there. He learned two things that I believe may very well be related: (1) they were leaving all their money, which was a considerable amount, to TBN, and (2) no one from the church had visited them in twenty years.

Sending money to help Sudanese refugees is, of course, a good thing, but I am seriously skeptical about how much of the money people send in is actually used for that purpose and how much is used to fund Parsley's lifestyle. There's a partial answer in a message that appears for exactly three and a half seconds at the end of his broadcast. The following disclaimer flashes on the screen:

> Disclaimer: This program originates from Breakthrough Studios at World Harvest Church, Columbus, Ohio. It is made possible through the prayerful support of Covenant Partners and Friends in this viewing area. Gifts are considered without restriction as to use unless specifically specified by the donor. Gifts designated to the Bridge of Hope projects will be used exclusively for the exempt purposes of Bridge of Hope.

Three and a half seconds, not nearly long enough to read and comprehend the fact that *you* have to specify that you want the money you send to be spent only in relief work. I certainly didn't notice it until I rewatched a recording of the show and even then I had to hit "pause" to be able to read it.

Advertisement: The Shadow of the Apocalypse: When All Hell Breaks Loose, by Paul Crouch with a foreword by Hal Lindsey ($12.95).

THE ROUNDUP

Old Testament passages cited: Three, plus his own retelling of Exodus.

New Testament passages cited: Zero.

Cost of products offered: $79.95–$1,037.95

Running total after 3½ hours: $843.94

God: Not mentioned too much except that God will release a sevenfold blessing to those who give money.

Jesus: Said the name once as a talisman.

Thought for this half-hour: Should our concern for those who suffer be elevated if they too are Christian?

Today with Marilyn and Sarah
(*I didn't know stickers could do that*)
8:30 a.m.

My guest Ted Pearlman was born in New York City and raised in New Jersey. Somewhere in the middle he apparently traveled the world with his parents, though he thinks the photos are fakes. He's an avid musician, community builder, pain-in-the-ass to his wife, and certified atheist-Jew. His basic feeling about religion is that if God is knowable, then he/she/it is not nearly sophisticated enough to be behind the wheel of the universe. He prefers the moniker "Nonbeliever in Awe."

◆◆◆

As Michael leaves, Ted, my just arrived viewing buddy, says to me: "So you're only on hour four, right? I expect your wit to be razor sharp." No pressure.

I met Ted when Matthew and I were looking into co-housing in Denver. Ted's the founder of a co-housing community and your basic everyday force of nature. I'm just grateful to have somebody here besides another Lutheran, and Ted couldn't be less Lutheran, so that's good. He actually shows up wearing a yarmulke (entirely for my benefit, not piety). "Hello. My name is Ted" is handwritten on a construction paper yellow star pinned to his shirt. In his hand is a kid's keep-busy-in-temple plaything, "My Jewish Activity Kit," which contains a toy Torah scroll. He sets it on the table and says "I brought some good reading in case I get bored." Ted's just wonderful enough to be delighted at being a Jew watching an hour of televangelism with his progressive Lutheran friend. He goes straight to the table of food I've set out for my guests and proceeds to harass me about my shiksa blueberry bagels and strawberry cream cheese.

The *Today with Marilyn and Sarah* intro is noticeably lower budget than the previous shows, and the vapid bouncy theme song smacks of PBS children's programming more than preaching. I hope against hope that Marilyn and Sarah really *are* in huge purple dinosaur suits, but once again I'm disappointed. They are a mother-daughter team in power suits. Ted and I miss most of the intro but tune in when Marilyn (the mother) says, "We love you. We care about you and more than anything you have a heavenly father who is deeply concerned about every need you have."

Ted: "Great! I'd love it if he could hook me up with a schmeer of normal cream cheese please."

Sarah is introducing the lesson she has for us today, but I can't hear her actual words because I'm completely distracted by the fact that she sounds exactly like a not-funny evangelical Paula Poundstone. Ted agrees.

"Hey, I know," Ted says, "let's close our eyes and pretend it's Paula Poundstone. It'll make it more fun." I resist the suggestion, so we're stuck with reality. Again.

Her sermon is titled "Passing God's Tests with Flying Colors."

Sarah uses the Genesis story to make the point that God tested Abraham and God tests us, so if you want to know how to pass these tests from God, ask, "What would Abraham do?"

Cut to Sarah preaching.

Her hair is spiky. She's in a Coca-Cola T-shirt and a faded denim jacket. I'm a little confused because a moment ago she was all Ann Taylor Loft on a Pottery Barn sofa with her mom, but now she's "hip" in a painfully constructed way. The camera pans back to show her entire profile and my confusion deepens. She's in polyester slacks, which are just a touch too short, and mom shoes. The Coca-Cola shirt looks as though it's over a lacy blouse. Was the whole T-shirt and denim jacket thing an illustration of an earlier sermon we didn't see, or was she late to the taping and only had time to put on the top half of her "hip preacher" uniform? The whole thing is really throwing me.

Me: "Look how 'relevant' she's trying to look."

Ted: "It's like Valerie Bertinelli meets the Sears catalog."

Sarah's using the Abraham story to talk about how we can come through tests from God. Here's her anagram:

T: Trust God — Abraham trusted God.

E: Engage in the process — Abraham built the altar to sacrifice Isaac.

S: Supply yourself (with the right resources) — Abraham took two servants and wood with him.

T: Time — It took three days for Abraham to get to the place for the sacrifice, so be patient.

Advertisement: Marilyn hocking a CD of her teaching *Dealing with Daddy's Demons* (which sounds more like an illegal dirty movie than an inspirational sermon) along with her book *Victorious Spiritual Warfare:*

These will help you stand fast against demonic activity and win. [But wait!] I have something so much fun ... a sticker you put on the bottom of your shoe [image of a red devil, pitchfork, horns, tail, the whole deal circled by a black international banned sign] to stomp out the devil and have victorious spiritual warfare.

There's nothing for me to add to that. It's a $30 "gift" for book, CD, and devil-stomping sticker. I wonder how much for just the stomp-out-the-devil stickers? They'd make killer stocking stuffers for my friends.

◆◆◆

Back to Sarah:

#1 Prepare. If you are not in a test, you will be soon. When God tests you it is not only so you can learn who he is, but also it is to prepare you for the next level of spiritual promotion.

Even Pelagius (fifth-century monk who believed we could all climb a spiritual ladder just by the force of our will and innate goodness) wouldn't like this. I have to admit, even though I don't believe in progressive sanctification, the idea of getting a spiritual promotion is actually pretty appealing. Would I stop being so self-referential and impatient after my spiritual promotion? Would I have that "I'm close to God" glow? Maybe a spiritual promotion would give my skin a more youthful sheen. Then I realize that if I am equating spiritual progress with better skin tone, then I perhaps am beyond help. My own we-cannot-by-our-own-efforts-climb-higher theology is pretty comforting to people like myself who are painfully aware of how much they would need a "spiritual promotion" if there were such a thing. How depressing would it be if, after exhausting all the steps and plans and secrets sold by TBN in book and CD sets, I was every bit as broken as I was to begin with?

Actually, maybe she's not so bad. Sarah just talked about how she's so stressed out right now and ready to go on vacation. Yesterday in the pastor's meeting she was short and snappy with her co-workers. That's her weak spot in times of stress, to be a little bitchy (my paraphrase). In almost five hours this is the first self-deprecation I've heard that was not located in the preacher's distant past when he or she "used to be" a sinner. She might not be a great preacher, but at least she's willing to admit that she's not perfect, which makes her that much closer to perfect in my twisted mind.

#2 Resource yourself. Memorize a few extra verses. That gives your mind an alternative. Resource yourself with extra prayer and the right people.

She's saying the same thing over and over.

#3 Engage with your test.
   When I am tested I will come out with gold.
   If you do not have Jesus in your life it is like taking a test with no teacher. Bench pressing with no spotter. Competing with no coach.

◆◆◆

Done. Back to Marilyn in a studio:

> Have you ever considered the significance of the number seven in the Bible? It is an awesome number. As I have studied the Gospel of John, I have discovered that there are seven "I am's" and each one had to do with a miracle.

She goes on to equate each "I am" in John with a miracle of Jesus. This is the first time I've heard anyone really talk much about Jesus, and I'm kind of impressed — until I realize that this whole thing is just a setup for a pitch. (And I feel suckered once again. What's up with my learning curve?)

> I want to send you my book *John: The Gospel of Real Life* plus three DVDs if you sow a seed of $70. There are seven special miracles waiting for you. When you send that $70 seed, that number of perfection, I will pray three special things just for you: that you will know God's purpose for your life, that God will bless a special act of obedience, and that he will give you one creative idea. Sow your seed today and expect your harvest.

> Ted: "What is this kind of Christianity called?"
> Me: "I have no idea."

THE ROUNDUP

Old Testament passages cited: Seven.

New Testament passages cited: One.

Cost of products offered: $100

Running total after 4 hours: $943.94

God: Sets up lots of tests and trials for you so that you can see who he is and earn a spiritual promotion.

Jesus: No mention (except in the ad to get people to sow a $70 seed).

Believer's Voice of Victory
(*"The Secret," televangelist-style*)
9:00 a.m.

An announcer opens the show with, "Join Gloria Copeland for a message about increase and how prosperity is just one instrument God uses to help us reach our full potential."

For the love of God, please let's hear something different. This "sowing seed," "love gift," and "increase" talk differs very little from the content filling my spam folder. Only "make your woman happy" seems to be missing.

Gloria stands behind a Plexiglas pulpit. She's an attractive older woman in a smart-looking suit, although her face appears to be stretched to within an inch of it's life.

Ted: "If it weren't for these evangelical preachers, the Plexiglas industry would go under."

The "Kenneth Copeland Ministries" banner looms large behind her — a world map with a huge "Jesus is Lord" scrolled across. To the left is an American flag and to the right is a flag with which I am unfamiliar. Absent are any symbols of the faith.

This is not the first flag we have seen on stage with a preacher. For some reason it just kind of blends in with the rest of this prosperity gospel aesthetic, but the truth is that if you go into many Lutheran churches, you'll find old glory in the sanctuary right next to the cross as though one completes the other. American flags were brought into German Lutheran churches during World War II to show where the German American community's loyalty lay. However, the origin of the practice has long since been forgotten, and now the flag is a seemingly permanent fixture in many of our churches. Matthew feels that having the flag in the sanctuary confuses the primary symbols of our faith. But, hey, who wants to be the guy who removes the American flag? He's pretty sure he'd get less flack if he removed the cross rather than the flag because, let's face it, people are more emotionally connected to the stars and stripes as a symbol.

Gloria is preaching at a pastor's conference:

Today we're going to talk about tithing. Attitude is everything with God. If you have a bad attitude, if you're doing what God wants you to do but you have a bad attitude about it, the blessing's not going to take hold like it should. The same thing is true with your sowing and harvest. If you're not sowing in joy, you're sowing in unbelief. Attitude is everything with God, if you can't do it in joy, you're probably not going to get a reward. Amen?

Me: "Oh, my gosh. This is Rhonda Byrne's *The Secret* evangelical style. Just believe and it will come to you." Gloria:

When you know the word of God, it's easy to expect from your tithe. Don't just write your check and plunk it in the plate. Put some faith behind it. Everything, in order to produce, has to have faith behind it. Every offering you give, pray over it, release it to the Lord, believe God for the return and harvest over that seed and do it in cheerfulness. It's going to cost you the same whether you are happy about it or sad.

Ted: "Are these people aware that they are predatory or are they so buried in their own mythology?"

◆◆◆

Growing up I remember my mom saying, "Tithing isn't God's way of raising money; it's God's way of raising children." We were raised to believe that all we had belonged to God, but the good news is that we get to keep 90 percent of it. We weren't giving away 10 percent of what was ours; we were keeping 90 percent of what wasn't ours to begin with. If tithing is about holding loosely what we have been given and the knowledge that it belongs to God and not to us, then giving it in order that we might get more in return seems counterproductive. How is that not simple greed? What I personally get back when I tithe is freedom from that particular amount of money; I no longer have to worry about losing it or wasting it. After getting rid of some money, I am no longer in danger of using it to indulge myself. I am no longer in danger of making a bad decision about how best to use it. Now the money is released. If it came back to me, but in greater quantity, I'd have to start all over again. This is not to say that I transcend materialism and love of money — far from it actually. I love money and I really love the stuff it buys, but I am painfully aware of this fact and tithing gives me a little freedom from this bondage to self. It is a small step toward keeping me right-sized, which isn't easily done, let me tell you.

She talks about how she and Ken had so little but "honored God" and "gained increase."

God can afford you. I don't care if you tithe 100 million dollars a day, he can open the window of heaven's tremendous increase upon that tithe. Glory to God! When you know what the Bible says you get excited.

I find the following part of the Bible exciting: "Beware and be on your guard against every form of greed; for not even when one has an abundance does his life consist of his possessions" (Luke 12:15). Gloria:

You just have to be smart enough to know that God knows more than you do. The Lord says I can be his if I choose to speak right words before him, if I choose to believe him and to honor him with my actions and my words, I can be his. It's my decision.

So God is smarter than us. Agreed. A problem with the "name it and claim it" theology is that human beings end up being the ones with all the agency. God wants to be active in the world, but God's hands are tied until we say and do the right things. This is deeply depressing to me.

Please, please let it not be true that God's work in the world depends on my thinking, saying, and doing all the right things because if so God wouldn't get a whole lot done, let me tell you. Gloria:

> Now that we've been redeemed from the curse, tithing should work more powerfully than it did in the old covenant because sin's been dealt with permanently. I'm not a sinner anymore; I am born again. Ken and I decided to do what the Bible says and that doesn't take a brain surgeon to figure out.

I beg to differ. You may know the words and speak the language and have perfect hair and manicure and southern accent, but you, Gloria, are a sinner. You are as broken and self-centered as I am.

Obviously if Matthew and I were super-duper into money, we'd not be Lutheran pastors. The starting salary out of seminary is about $27,000 plus a 30 percent housing allowance. So $35,500 before taxes. There are times when it gets to us. For people with master's degrees we make very little money, which means there are things we cannot afford to do. We don't take fancy vacations; our children are not in riding lessons and dance class. But in the end our needs are always met in a loaves-and-fishes sort of way. Somehow every time we have a huge dental bill or our cars need work, money is provided. I have no good explanation for this; all I know is that it happens. Still, when Matthew's seventeen-year-old Subaru dies, I have no idea how we'll manage, only that we will.

THE ROUNDUP

Old Testament passages cited: Twelve

New Testament passages cited: Zero

Cost of products offered: CD of this week's broadcast: $10; DVD: $15.

Running total after 4½ hours: $968.94

God: Just sits around waiting for us to do the right thing with the right attitude so that he can shower us with cash and prizes. This is the game show God.

Jesus: Who?

Thought for this half-hour: God can afford me (but maybe not you).

Postscript: My Sister Emails in Solidarity

My sister, in an act of support and solidarity, was watching some TBN at her house while I was at mine. Soon after *Believer's Voice of Victory* ended, she sent me this email:

◆◆◆

I could only manage to stomach half an hour of TBN, even given the deep love I have for you, dear sister. They better be paying you big bucks to watch a full day's worth of this stuff. I watched the last part of Marilyn Hickey and then most of Gloria Copeland.

MH was trying to get people to "sow a seed of $70" because seven is the perfect number and Jesus said seven different "I Am's" (so why not sow a seed of $7? Wouldn't that be better?). She would pray three prayers of great significance for each sower of a seed of $70 (only three? I thought *seven* was the perfect number . . . hmmm). I think my husband would very much like to heed her admonition, and I quote her directly: "I encourage you to sow your seed today." But if he did that, he'd be raising three out-of-control children all alone, because, well, if there's any seed sowing to be done, he'd better not be looking at sowing it in *her* field.

Interestingly (or maybe predictably — this is the only TBN I've ever seen in my life), Gloria Copeland was "preaching" on sowing as well. Copeland was arguing that you have to tithe with a good attitude because "the blessings aren't going to take hold like they should" if you are sad about letting the 10 percent go to the Lord. She said, "Do it in faith, or the blessing can't come on ya," and at another time she said, "That's the way you get delivered and stay delivered." The use of passive voice here is so telling, isn't it? The focus is on what you can do to "get delivered." The person with faith is obviously the agent of everything in life, and God is relegated somehow to the role of a puppet who will raise his hands or feet if we pull the string *in faith* (of course).

The implications, in terms of compassion and Christ-likeness and condemnation of others, are immense. If the Christian life really is all about pulling those puppet strings in faith, about living a victorious life, and about "getting delivered and staying delivered," then what is the obvious attitude toward the person who is still in poverty or illness or who continues to be burdened by besetting sin? Are we to despise that person for lacking faith when faith is a gift of God and not of our own doing, so that no man should boast?

I thought, too, that it was so interesting how sowing means money to these people. I honestly had never thought of the parable of the sower in monetary terms.

I'd be interested in hearing if you experienced that hostage syndrome, where you start to take on the side of your kidnappers, sympathizing with them after they have held you captive for so many hours. What hour did it begin to seem reasonable to you, all that they said?

Good luck with the project. I love you. — B

Best of Praise the Lord
(*Siegfried and Roy go to Burning Man*)
9:30 a.m.

Like many of my guests, Ted has stayed on past his time slot.

Praise the Lord is a Christian talk show, and today Mark Chironna Hosts Dyan Cannon. I vaguely remember her; I think she was the judge on *Ally McBeal.*

The decorating is faux everything. Huge fake plants, enormous fake Louis XVI furniture, and white and gold walls. It's very Siegfried and Roy meets Tammy Faye — absolute prosperity gospel heaven. Is there something righteous about the faux ornate, just as there seems to be an implied righteousness, here on TBN, to certain hair styles and music and manicures and decorating? There's an evangelical aesthetic of righteousness. Even the music is faux: it's piped in.

Ted notices, "The set looks like the shrapnel from a Hobby Lobby explosion."

"There's something to that," I offer, "because Hobby Lobby is owned by evangelical Christians. They may actually be providing this Look of Righteousness."

The show opens with a schmaltzy praise song: "Abba Father."

Praise music makes my skin crawl. I'm not against giving praise to God, just against doing it with vapid bad soft rock. There's a great episode of the animated sitcom *King of the Hill* in which thirteen-year-old Bobby joins a Christian rock band. His dad, Hank, says, "Bobby, you're not making Christianity better, son. You're just making rock and roll worse." I'm with Hank.

Dyan Cannon looks amazing, but her long curly flowing blond hair and unlined face look like they belong to someone decades younger. Perhaps they're on loan. Several strands of beads cover her neck and leather pants cover her slim legs.

Ted: "I'm fascinated that she has jewelry covering the areas that can't be botoxed, like her neck is the demilitarized zone."

She's like an evangelical vixen, which I find refreshing after hours of helmet hair and power suits. She's got the face of a thirty-year-old and the body of a twenty-year-old, but suddenly it dawns on me . . . wait, wasn't Dyan Cannon married to Cary Grant at one point? He was born in 1902 so she's not young. I Google her to find out her age. Surely the date on the Internet has to be wrong; there's no way she was born in 1937. But if she was, she's seventy. Now I'm completely freaked out. Perhaps she's from another planet. I accept that theory for the moment and try to put her freakish appearance out of my mind.

When asked why she's so radical for Jesus, Cannon replies:

The world dangles carrots in front of us, this one is fame, this one is wealth, this one is men. And tells you they will make you happy. Well I had them all, and I wasn't happy. I tried everything the world had to offer except Him, and that black hole inside me just kept getting deeper, and deeper but now I'm full [of collogen and botox].

◆◆◆

Her community is called God's Party, which sounds great, but she mentions that they sometimes sing and praise for hours, which sounds like torture.

Ted: "Do you think God's Party might be like Burning Man, but like, in a church in Pasadena or something?"

Burning Man is a Power Pagan event held in the California desert each year: nakedness, debauchery, the complete suspension of the cash economy, and lighting really big things on fire. I like to imagine Ted is right.

Dyan: "If we'd just for a minute take that mask off and let it all hang out, there can be an incredible healing presence. This was not my plan; this all came in such a surprising way. If he can use me, he can use anybody because I was at the bottom of a pit, and he lifted me up. I needed to be repaired and that's ongoing."

Mark: "It's okay to admit we need to be repaired."

Dyan: "All the time."

◆◆◆

She's prays into the camera one of those creepy "Father God, I just want to…I just ask that…I just…prayers" and ends by saying, "You're such a wonderful papa." But I forgive that because she just admitted that she is a fractured person in need of God. Amen, sister. Me too. This I can get behind.

I'm feeling a bit wobbly now. That half-hour went by awfully quickly. I'm not sure if it's too much coffee, the five and a half hours I've watched so far, or the fact that I just got really into something said on TBN.

Ted: "I have to go. Would you like to keep the yellow star?"

Me: "More than anything in the world. Hey, you guys don't have anything like Jewish TV do you?"

Ted: "We generate our cash with other methods — like the saving of Israel."

Me: "Got it."

Mark Wase joins me. The two Jews on my guest list are somehow scheduled back to back, but Mark is a bit of a Jewtheran.

◆◆◆

My guest Mark Wase: I am a forty-two-year-old white male residing in Denver, Colorado.

I grew up in a middle- to upper-middle-class Jewish family in the suburbs of, and then central, Philadelphia. We were mildy practicing reform Jews; however, my mother was from an orthodox family (albeit a strange, hypcritical version), and Judaism was very present. My parents themselves were very open-minded and raised my sister and me to be the same. We were never told what to believe or whom to associate with, marry, etc. We were indeed taught love and tolerance to all.

Despite my parents' best efforts (and also to other degrees *with* their influence!) I became a highly dysfunctional alcoholic, ADD-riddled degenerate, and, by the time I was twenty, an everyday drunk with nasty gambling and drug habits. This continued until I was thirty-two, at which time I had a bit of an epiphany moment and started sobering up and following a road of recovery. I have not had a drink or drug since April 21, 1998, and have experienced a spiritual rebirth (with varying degrees of success and failure along the way!) within this journey.

AA sparked my spiritual awakening, and due to personal angst toward the Jewish religion (some deserved and some not so deserved), I have experimented with various types of participation in organized religion — none of which have been even remotely related to Judaism. For whatever reasons (which I could certainly expound on but do not have the time, discipline, or space to do so here) I have felt most comfortable with liberal but mainstream sects of Christianity, and when I do go to church it is usually of the liberal Lutheran variety. I do not go very often, maybe once every three months, but often aspire to going more.

◆◆◆

The next segment of *Praise the Lord* opens with a folksy song, "Pray for America." The audience sings along, a predominantly African American audience, which surprises me, but I'm not sure why. Maybe this God Bless America stuff just seems so "white" to me? The religious right seems to have an interesting lens for looking at the history of our country, namely, that the founding fathers were all Republican evangelicals à la George Bush. I assume that, not patriotism itself, but this rosy Christian, one-nation-under-Jesus view of American history would be more challenging to embrace for the descendants of slaves. But at least this particular *Praise the Lord* audience is willingly singing along.

Actually watching TV for hours at a time is going to be harder than I thought, especially when my friends are here. Mark and I end up chatting quite a bit about my time at Luther Seminary, the timing of my ordination, and the new house, and we're not really paying a lot of attention to the TV.

Okay, focus, focus.

An ad for the Holy Land Experience, TBN's ancient Holy Land theme park in Orlando, Florida, comes on. "Travel back two thousand years. Relive ancient Jerusalem at the Holy Land Experience," the narrator intones. Cut to a middle-aged white man in the midst of the amusement park claiming "95 percent of all learning is done through the eyes. You can read it and make some sense out of it, but when you actually see it, it really does impact you." Cut to reenactment of blowing a shofar, then to a Roman guard, then sandaled feet walking a cobbled path. "Walk the streets, feel the energy." Shot of a Fabio Jesus reenactment actor complete with well-trimmed beard, cloak, and boom mic. "Look into the eyes of the man who would change the course of history." White female guest: "the

Bible comes alive." Shots of a tabernacle reenactment including the Holy of Holies. "Discover the mystery of the wilderness tabernacle. Trace the meticulous efforts of the scribes." White middle-aged male guest: "It was an excellent historical overview of how we got our Bible."

"Broaden your knowledge and understanding. Take the journey. Explore the Holy Land Experience." Shot of a purple-cloaked actress gesturing graciously at the front gate. "It will change you forever."

◆◆◆

From the people who brought you Tammy Faye Bakker, a hyper-real* Jerusalem. What is most disturbing to me is the way the language of the ad implies that the Holy Land Experience is really the Holy Land. The guest who said that you can understand the Bible only once you see it seems entirely unaware that he isn't seeing the Bible, or ancient Jerusalem, or Jesus himself for that matter, but a simulacrum. Ancient Jerusalem doesn't exist, but in a world in which every aspect of our lives is saturated with media and simulation, the difference between what is real (the Bible) and what is hyper-real (the reenactment of the Bible) is blurred beyond distinction. The ad suggests that at the Holy Land Experience we can "look into the eyes of the man who would change the course of history." I'm sure the Jesus reenactment actor, let's call him Steve, is a nice enough guy, but I'm not convinced that Steve is going to change the course of history (but hey, I've been wrong before).

Fancy French philosopher Jean Baudrillard calls Disneyland (arguably the godfather of the Holy Land Experience) "the first great toxic excrement of a hyper-real civilization." The Holy Land Experience, while perhaps not the second great toxic excrement, is up there somewhere.

Advertisement: Your love gift this month will help TBN send the gospel around the world. [They read an excerpt from a deployed serviceman in Iraq thanking them that he gets to hear God's word on Sundays and to please pray for him. A collage of American soldiers follows while "God Bless the USA" plays in the background.]

◆◆◆

The next segment of *Praise the Lord* opens with a snappy southern gospel tune about Joshua and the walls of Jericho sung by a woman who looks like Marie Osmond in big hair and a bad suit. Okay, so just like Marie Osmond, pre-*Dancing with the Stars.*

---

*Hyper-real: a reality by proxy in which the simulation becomes more real than the actual reality.

Our host this half-hour is an older African American man, and the celebrity guest is Debra Paget, who (thank you, Google) played Lilia in Cecil B. De Mille's *Ten Commandments,* which she says was a film that "brought so many people to God." I personally found the combination of white folks playing Egyptians and Charlton Heston's acting to be almost fatal.

Advertisement: Fabergé-style egg (which houses a miniature Holy Family within its jewel-like belly) ($250). I'll take two.

TBN's "Praise-a-thon" is coming up. Paul Crouch Jr. is on-screen claiming that TBN doesn't "shove advertising down your throat" but that they raise funds like churches do — by passing the basket. He's pitching TBN's latest endeavor, *Second Chance:* "A satellite dish in every U.S. prison. The 2 million American incarcerated represent a huge mission field."

"This is something we've already been doing for quite some time in the Soviet U . . . er . . . in Russia. Ninety percent of prisons in Russia get a TBN feed." Ouch.

He's asking viewers who might know someone in prison to call and help get TBN into U.S. prisons. "Sometimes it's not what you know; it's who you know." Well, *I* know my brother who is the head psychologist in a federal prison, so I call him up to see if his fellas watch TBN. Apparently there's no way I'd get an official statement from a federal employee, but let's just say that maybe he talked to a chaplain there who maybe said that they would never even consider allowing TBN in the prison because maybe TBN is predatory. I wonder too about how wise it is to telecast anti-Muslim rhetoric into American prisons. Those quaint little "Thank you for converting me to Christianity. Love, Mohammed" letters that Paul Crouch loves to read on this show might not go over so well.

◆◆◆

I ask Mark about his reactions to the evangelical Christian God Bless America ethos on these programs.

Mark: "This seems like such a complete manipulation of the flock and makes me question the validity of the whole thing. It feels like a real lack of spirituality in evangelical Christianity because it seems like such a manipulative use of authority. They are taught that the laws of God and the laws of the land are the same thing, but the laws of the land follow a political agenda rather than a spiritual agenda, and these people use the flock to get power. I think 70 percent of the Republicans in Congress have most of their funding through an evangelical base and with it has been a gradual erosion of civil liberties. They've quietly given the executive branch the power to erode the separation between church and state. That's a new thing — the direction being toward less civil rights rather than more. This includes the marriage amendments."

Me: "It's as though they say that America is sacred in the very same way that Jesus is sacred, so your loyalty to America is interchangeable with your loyalty to Jesus and vice versa. These people rock the vote because that type of language spawns a whole different order of commitment. So Mark, if the religious right is the dominant image of Christianity out there, then why are you attracted to this faith as someone who was raised Jewish?"

Mark: "The dominant image doesn't have to be my image. I'm drawn through necessity, through the depths of alcoholism, and I had to be "saved" from that in some way. I found myself with a desire to pray in community without it being an AA meeting. I don't feel comfortable in Judaism. It gives me the hives, just like recovering Catholics and I don't feel comfortable in synagogue. I identify with the heritage, but I also get hives when I go to the Orthodox synagogue, where women sit separately from men. It's a real turn off. I went to an evangelical community church a couple of times, but if I thought that was the whole thing, that that was all Christianity was about, I'd never want anything to do with it. But I went to Lutheran churches that had gay ministers, and I had no idea they could be so accepting. I just feel the TBN types have hijacked the Christian agenda and people."

Ann Coulter is up next on *Behind the Scenes*. This should be fun.

THE ROUNDUP

Old Testament passages cited: Zero.

New Testament passages cited: Zero.

Cost of products offered: $250.

Running total after 5 hours: $1218.94

God: Papa can you hear me?

Thought for this hour and a half: I hope I look as good as Dyan Cannon when I'm seventy-one. Oh wait, I don't look that good *now* and I'm thirty-eight.

Behind the Scenes
(*Liberals in heaven?*)
11:00 a.m.

News-like intro; spinning globe, international flags, typewriter-like sounds.

Announcer: "This is a *Behind the Scenes* international report with founder Paul Crouch. Join us for Paul's around-the-world daily report to you, our partners."

I'm alone for a few minutes and take the opportunity to splash some water on my face. These first hours have whizzed by; with a little luck I'll actually make it through. In fact it's fun: this weird thing where interesting people come to my house all day to watch televangelism. I'm not saying I'd do it again in a few days, but so far it's kind of a kick.

◆◆◆

On screen TBN's executive director Paul Crouch Jr. sits among a set of blue chairs that look as though they were built within the imagination of Lewis Carroll. Behind him is the obligatory city nightscape complete with fake palm trees. He's filling in for his dad on this TBN show about TBN.

Again PC Jr. mentions their upcoming fundraising week. I didn't know until I started watching for twenty-four hours that there would be no typical commercial breaks. All of the advertising on TBN (and there is plenty) is for TBN-related products and services, so I feel like I can't just tune that out. This causes a bit of a problem when one has committed to write a book about watching twenty-four consecutive hours of TBN. Until hour one I had assumed that I'd get a break from the religious programming every eight or nine minutes. Instead, it never stops. Normally I would be all for a dearth of car ads and talking GEICO lizards, but now after six hours of nonstop Christian preaching and pitches, preaching and pitches, would a Palmolive commercial kill them?

◆◆◆

PC Jr. introduces a clip called "What is TBN"? I'm excited, as I am currently asking myself the very same question, so I look forward to the clarity I'm certain this will bring. We start with a closeup of two matches being struck and growing into a flame (representing founders Paul and Jan Crouch?).

PC Jr.:

One light can brighten a small area and multiply into a light for all to see. So it is with the ministry of TBN. A ministry that goes into

59

your city and around the world. [Shot of Jan and Paul from thirty-four years ago.] TBN started as a small local channel in southern California, and grew into a network of stations [U.S. map littered with dots, then a shot of a Bedouin on a camel riding past the Great Pyramids], branched into foreign lands, and now literally to the ends of the earth.

In the United States TBN spreads the gospel through over-the-air television stations in major cities, a vast cable network, home satellite service, over the Internet, and through new technology systems like podcasting. On TBN you'll see the best in inspirational and Christian programming, our flagship program *PTL*, variety programs, music, movies, drama, health and nutrition, sports, reality series, as well as the best in preaching and teaching [shows a short clip of an African American preacher, shouting, "Get out of the way"] — all part of what makes TBN the most watched inspirational network in the United States. To reach an even broader audience, TBN has launched four more U.S. networks: the Church Channel, the Spanish-language ENLACE, a youth channel called JC TV, and for our youngest viewers, Smile of a Child.

Jesus commanded us to take the gospel into all of the world, and TBN is using the powerful tool of television to do just that; sixty-four satellites and thousands of television and cable stations blanket Europe, Africa, Asia, and South America, and entire TBN networks offer twenty-four-hour programming in Spanish, Italian, Russian, Arabic, and Farsi. As a result, billions of people, including many in harsh anti-Christian societies, can receive the gospel, can receive salvation, encouragement, and hope. [As this is said a series of images of people around the globe in typical native garb with big TBN smiles on their faces flash by.] Sowing into good ground should result in a harvest, and TBN has borne much fruit.

Millions have called in to receive Jesus. [You can receive Jesus by calling in? Could I just send a text? Would that do the job?] And letters and emails pour in from around the world with testimonies of salvation, healing, and changed lives. [They now cut to a clip of Paul Crouch on *PTL* reading a letter from Iran.] "To God be the Glory, we just had an incredible conversion. One of our phone counselors just led one of the top Islamic leaders to the Lord' [audience goes wild; cue triumphalist music].

Our television stations, cable systems, satellites, the Internet — all fed twenty-four hours a day with innovative, creative, soul-winning programs, all supported by you. Our partners, join us in touching the world — person by person, city by city, nation by nation to the ends of the earth. Call now and be a part of Praise-a-thon 2007.

So *that* is how TBN views itself.

Paul Crouch Jr. is hosting Ann Coulter, who describes herself as "a Christian first and a mean-spirited, bigoted Republican second." She's promoting her new book *If Democrats Had Any Brains They'd Be Republicans*. I honestly adore her. She's beautiful, smart, and funny. She's wrong, but I think she's great because at least she is bold. Who's the left's Ann Coulter? Is it Al Franken? He's great, but why does the right have a leggy blond and the left a middle-aged Jew from Minnesota?

Ann's wearing a tasteful black sweater set and a cross necklace. This new book is mostly a collection of her so-called "career ending statements" or something, as she describes it, "for liberals who want to hate me but don't have much time to read." She's hoping that the book will, besides making liberals want to spit nails, inspire young conservatives coming up so that they too can speak with such vitriol and know it's okay.

When PC Jr. asks Ann if while compiling the material for the book she had maybe forgotten she'd actually said some of these things, she says "Yes, and then I thought, 'that's brilliant, totally magnificent.' " This makes me laugh, until I find myself distracted from the conversation by Ann Coulter's Adam's apple.

She remembers after her family moved to Connecticut her mother stopped going to the local Presbyterian church for awhile because the sermons were political — denouncing the Vietnam war. "That is not what most Christians want out of church; it's certainly not what my mother wanted. It drove her away. She still believed in God and was an absolutely wonderful Christian; she just stopped going to that church."

I find her assertion that Christians don't want to hear politics in church to be ironic considering the power of the religious right. Perhaps she means that Christians don't want to hear about peace and social justice "politics" in church, only pro-life, pro-war, pro-business "politics."

Ann is so fun on her own without my having to say a thing that for the rest of this session I have disabled my own comments. Ladies and gentlemen, I give you Ann Coulter:

"One thing liberals attack me for, because they are so biblically ignorant, is they start investigating whether I really go to church, which for one thing I do, and for another thing we don't have to go to church; we're Christian. Christ died for our sins. What a religion!"

"I love campaigns because we get to see the Democrats faking a belief in God."

PC Jr.: "How should Christians vote?"
Ann: "With whoever is pro: small government, national security, and life."

PC Jr.: "What about the Democratic side?"
Ann: "They're bad."
PC Jr.: "There will be Democrats in heaven you know."
Ann: "Zell Miller, Pat Caddell . . . that pretty much rounds it out."

PC Jr.: "When you pray at night, what do you pray?"
Ann: "That God will smite liberals" [laughs]. "That's a little Christian humor. I pray for my friends and family."
PC Jr.: "God listens to Ann Coulter?"
Ann: "Well, I just think he was really happy I mentioned him on CNBC."

◆◆◆

It just would have been obvious and silly for me to add anything.

The segment ends with a time filler clip of a biblical reenactment: Jesus walking on water. A storm rages while the terrified disciples cower in their little boat. Peter dares to give it a go, and he too steps out onto the water. He does okay for a few steps but then "loses faith" and begins to sink. I have to say, I saw that coming.

THE ROUNDUP

Old Testament passages cited: Zero.

New Testament passages cited: Zero.

Cost of products offered: $250 for a Fabergé-style egg. I'll take three.

Running total after 6½ hours: $1468.94

God: Republican.

Jesus: Grateful for any level of press coverage.

Thought for this half-hour: I hope Ann Coulter and I will sit at the same dinner table in heaven.

Paula White Today
[again, sigh, see page 11]
(Forgetting about kangaroos)
11:30 a.m.

My guest Paul Moeller is the Bibliographer for Religious Studies for the University Libraries at the University of Colorado at Boulder. He was raised Roman Catholic but is nonreligious.

◆◆◆

I soon realize that I now have to watch the same Paula White episode from 5:30 a.m. Whether this feels more merciful or punitive is unclear at this point. Paul is here so I'll get to see his reactions to Ms. White. In the interest of fairness, I should try to keep my own opinions about Paula (for instance that she might be the devil) to myself and just see what Paul thinks.

I make it one full minute before telling Paul all my thoughts about Paula: her "nail gestures," her silly little Anglo-Saxon word study, her low-brow theological glossolalia. So much for not contaminating the experiment.

As she talks about how we are to worship continually and that we are to think of God all the time, I'm reminded of when my daughter Harper, four at the time, sat at the dinner table looking pensive until finally saying, "Mom, sometimes I forget about kangaroos." To which I replied, "Honey, we all do. It would be exhausting to continually remember kangaroos." I'm pretty sure that no one can think about God *or* kangaroos all the time. I can't even manage to be thinking about TBN continually for one day, and it's right in front of my face.

◆◆◆

As we watch Paula parse English into theological profundities, Paul's predictably skeptical of her "loving Jesus fixes all one's relationship problems" line and the determined vagueness of what the various thanks offerings requested by Paula will go to. Paul remains unconverted.

THE ROUNDUP

Old Testament passages cited: Nine.

New Testament passages cited: Eight.

Thought for this half-hour: Try to always think of God. . . . Oh, look, something sparkly . . . damn.

63

Life Today
(*In the down-homey log cabin of millionaires*)
12:00 p.m.

Announcer: "Keep tuned as James and Betty share their story of hope beyond hurt on *Life Today*."

"We are in a set that we asked our ministry leadership to build for us," James Robison, a kindly man in his sixties tells us. He had asked them to "prepare a place where we could come in and just talk heart to heart with you; we felt we needed to be able to talk directly to you. We get calls from people who have high-impact testimonies who are flying through the Dallas airport, and they could just come and talk to us."

The set looks like a spacious log cabin: fireplace, wood floor, rustic pine furniture, the works. James and Betty are dressed casually; he in jeans, tennis shoes, and a button-down shirt, she in a simple white shirt and cardigan. But it is their Texas voices that really say "down home casual." Gone is the glitz and capped teeth of Paula White. These are some regular folks. James says, "Betty and I want to share with you. Now I want you to listen very closely as though we're sitting right there close to you."

I turn to Paul. "These two seem more like regular people, I mean compared to some of the others on here."

To which he replies, "Nadia, are you serious? That's what they're trying to do. He just said, 'We built this set so that it will feel like we're right there with you.' That's the point, to come off as homey and safe."

Well, now I feel like a sucker.

Pulling out an old cardboard suitcase not much bigger than a large briefcase, James tells the story of how, when he was five years old, he had to leave his adopted home with the Rev. and Mrs. Hale. He was born in the charity ward to a forty-year-old home health care worker who was raped by the son of her client; James claims to be the "result of a forced sexual relationship." He lived with the Hales, the pastor of the church Betty grew up in, for the first five years of his life. Then at age five his mother came and dragged him away. He spent the next ten years living in extreme poverty, moving from place to place with his mother. He used that suitcase to sit on while he and his mother hitchhiked across country. James speaks of being grateful for those years of hardship and pain because they have helped to give him a "heart to help the suffering." When James was fifteen his alcoholic father entered the scene again and made their lives "a living hell." One evening, fearing for the lives of his mother and himself, James pulled a .30-06 on his father and told him, "If you move so much as a finger I'm going to blow a hole in you big enough for someone to crawl through." James continues:

> Now I want you to listen to me. [James is looking directly into the camera now.] You may have been exposed to religion, you may have watched some religious television and thought it was pretty hokey and spacey and wondered if it was real, and I understand that. But too many people are into religion and not into relationship. But that night with everything I had I went up and put the life of a teenage boy into the hands of God, and I know that that night God was pleased. Because I received God's son, with whom he was pleased. No one had ever been pleased with me before, but that night God became my father.
>
> Give him your life; release his light toward others. There's an 800 number on your screen. It's paid for by love, by those who love God. You call that number and say, "I've just prayed, and I need a new beginning. I need hope beyond hurt." Someone will pray with you.
>
> You know, Betty, we get calls and letters every day with viewers saying they want to know what work we're doing because they want to be a part of that, to be a part of God's heart [she nods lovingly as he now looks directly into the camera]. Here's what I want to ask you to do right now. I want you to be part of a Miracle in a Bowl, which gives 400,000 children and their families a chance at life. Won't you go to the phone right now and use your bank card like a check, give $30, $50, $100, or $1,000, to be a miracle.

A video montage of starving babies with flies on their faces and cups waiting for gruel is accompanied by a voice-over claiming that Life International's food reserves are depleted.

Paul: "Well at least there's an attempt to show what they'll do with the money. With Paula White, you just kind of send it in and you're saved."

I do a quick Internet search on Life Outreach, only to find that they list in their FAQs that Life Outreach strives to keep all costs to a minimum, while maximizing every gift for ministry and mission work. Life Outreach registers with the Better Business Bureau annually, but they don't mention that they fail to meet three of the BBB's financial standards for charity organizations. It took me all of two minutes to find this out, but I wonder if the folks who give the Robisons money have this information. I actually felt really moved by his story, and I kind of wish that his organization was on the up and up, because they really seemed so sweet and likable and now I feel like maybe I just fell for it like a sucker. They've gone from James's testimony to a relief plea — to music: a painfully earnest guy at a piano playing particularly heinous Christian singer-songwriter music, some guy named Michael O'Brian singing a song called "What Held You on the Cross?" Well, Michael, it wasn't duct tape, I'll tell you that much.

❖❖❖

Advertisement: With a gift of any amount: *Then Sings My Soul* CD. With $125 or more comes *Then Sings My Soul,* a book about the great hymns of the church. But wait! If you "prayerfully consider" giving a gift of $1,000 or more, they will give you a bronze sculpture of a mommy and baby deer titled "As the Deer. . . . "

I'd be more likely to give $1,000 for them *not* to send me a bronze deer sculpture, but that's beside the point.

THE ROUNDUP

Old Testament passages cited: Zero.

New Testament passages cited: Zero.

Cost of products offered: $30–$1,000 to be a "miracle"; $125–$1,000 for CD, book, and statue.

Running total after 7½ hours: $1623.94

Thought for this half-hour: Could some of these folks be legit?

Intermission

REFLECTION ON
THE BLANK SCREEN

The Grassley Six

I RECENTLY LISTENED to an NPR story about the ongoing Senate investigation of the so-called Grassley Six; Creflo and Taffi Dollar, Paula and Randy White, Eddie Long, Benny Hinn, Kenneth Copeland, and Joyce Meyer — prosperity gospel preachers whose 501c3 status is being questioned in light of the Bentleys and Leer jets being purchased with "nonprofit" funds from their respective churches.

As a Lutheran I reject wholesale the gospel of prosperity, primarily on the grounds that I'm pretty sure it makes Jesus throw up a little bit every time he thinks of it.

The NPR story opens with an audio clip of a Kenneth Copeland sermon, "This Is the Word Become Flesh, the Word Become Health and Healing, the Word Become Massive Wealth." How one goes from the "Word become flesh" — God entering fully into the muck of our existence in the scandal of an illegitimate child born in the filth of a barn, the Almighty slipping into skin in the most vulnerable and beautiful way possible — to "Word become massive wealth" is beyond me. Unless one ignores the entirety of all four gospels. None of us truly knows the mind of Christ, but my best guess is that he'd have something to say about this. We are left with precious few teachings from Jesus on many, many topics; wealth is not one of them. When Jesus spoke of wealth, it was cautionary at best, and at worst it was nearly condemning.

This is where things get uncomfortable. As I write snarky commentary about prosperity gospel preachers and how their lavish lifestyles are paid for primarily through the Social Security checks of the disempowered, I do so from the comfort of my 1948 brick ranch. My husband and I are a clergy couple, so everything we have is paid for by the donations of others: our two cars (old but paid for), my expensive jeans, his garage full of back country gear, the $3-a-dozen organic eggs in the fridge. All of it. I too live a lavish lifestyle funded by the giving of the faithful, and this realization is discomforting. It is undoubtedly the plank in my own eye.

This Is Your Day with Benny Hinn
(*Catching the mic in one smooth motion*)
12:30 p.m.

My guest Holly Heuer was born in Monroe, Louisiana, and was raised in the Presbyterian Church (US) — the "southern" Presbyterian Church. Her parents were church elders, and her three siblings are all presently active in the denomination. She graduated from Southern Methodist University with a degree in education and taught in the public schools in Dallas, Texas. Perceiving a "call" to ministry, she entered Austin Presbyterian Theological Seminary in 1975 and graduated with a master's of divinity degree. She has served

small congregations as pastor in Louisiana and Colorado and is currently serving Calvary Presbyterian Church in Denver. She received
her doctor of ministry degree at Iliff School of Theology and is ad-
junct professor there. Holly is married and has two children, two
stepchildren, and four grandchildren.

◆◆◆

Intro: a series of quick-cut fast-forwarded images, trains leaving station,
clocks spinning, etc.

Announcer: "Time: There is never enough. In fact, time is running
out."

Benny Hinn's voice: "Dangers have never been so high and our time
has never been so limited."

Clips of Hinn's massive crusades — stadiums from all over the world
filled with tens of thousands of people.

Announcer: "Benny Hinn is pressing toward the goal to win all the lost.
Man's greatest need is salvation through God's son Jesus Christ."

Benny: "The gift of God is life eternal. Today is your day to join us at
winning the lost at any cost."

◆◆◆

Me: "It's been obvious thus far today that when you're giving money
to them you are helping to save souls."

Matthew (as he walks through the living room): "Somebody recently
asked me if I was still in the soul-saving business. I told him that was never
my job; that's God's job. I just tell the story."

A San Jose stadium is filled with what must be fifty thousand people
raising their hands and singing. I wonder what came before to whip the
people into such a state. I know that in Lutheran churches it doesn't
happen as soon as they sit down and open the bulletin. (Okay, it never
actually happens in Lutheran churches.) Practically everyone is weeping,
swaying, and singing — all while keeping their eyes closed.

Holly: "There's a place for this. It's a first step that is radical and
positive, but you can then mature out of it."

It's good that Holly is here. I took a preaching class from her last spring
and was deeply impressed by her. She's spiritually spunky and seems to
have many things I lack, not the least of which is a total absence of
cynicism. I respect her so much that I'm really trying to bracket out my
own sarcasm and bitterness for the hour. If anyone can persuade me to see
this differently, it's Holly. There's something kind of pure but not perfect

about her; she's lovely but transparent enough that one can still see the broken bits.

"Arise and be healed in the name of Jesus," Benny intermittently repeats the words of the song over the crowd, but a bit slower and off key. "Call his name Jesus." Everyone sings "Jesus" while the organ plays.

We finally get the first closeup shot of Hinn in his classic white Nehru jacket emblazoned with the Benny Hinn Ministries logo: a gold dove.

"So many people are getting healed here today." The crowd sings and sings "He's the Savior of My Soul," while Hinn softly says "Jesus."

Holly observes, "One of the most important archetypes is the innocent — they give their lives over to a power or personality who will save them from this bad world. And we return again to this stage later but as an enlightened innocent."

"A second naiveté?"

"Yes. If we have entirely lost the innocent archetype, then we are completely cynical."

"Yeah," I confess, "for instance, when I'm in a worship service that includes praise music, I can't seem to overcome my cynicism long enough to experience anything other than the feeling of wanting to leave my body."

"You may want to look at your innocent. . . . "

My initial thought is "Um, no thanks," but I know she's right. I wonder about being the pastor of an emerging church and how so many of my people are really pretty cynical. I wonder if I can get to the point where I might be able to hold the innocence for them, so that they know it's okay.

"I never went through this stage either," Holly admits, then adding, "Well, when I was in fifth grade my boyfriend gave his life over to Jesus, and it was so sexual. What I mean is that you're just kind of blissing out."

The people sing in time and on key, and again Hinn repeats slower and off key. They seem to be all in a trance singing as a slow chant, "Jesus your presence makes me whole."

Holly: "That slow repeating chant is the same as what Taizé is doing with young people."

I love Taizé, a Christian monastic community in France to which thousands of young people pilgrimage each summer. Their music is simple, beautiful chant. I don't like the idea of associating something I like with something I don't, but now that she's said it I have no choice.

They sing and sing. "Jesus you're all I need," and Hinn says softly over and over, "Jesus. . . . "

Holly: "In the mainline we appeal only to people who have reached a certain maturity — wait, 'maturity' isn't right. What I mean is that we don't even honor this sort of experience at all."

She's right of course. I know for a fact that Lutherans are very suspicious of anything terribly emotive. We believe more in salvation through theological precision.

Suddenly they cut to a different part of the service. A large man in a pin-striped suit is standing near a homely, slightly disturbed-looking woman stage-right of Hinn. Holding a microphone he tells Hinn, "This lady had lupus. For twenty-two years she has had so much pain she couldn't even walk up the stairs." As he says this he points to this woman, who is now jumping up and down ready to run up the stage stairs. "She's been showing me that she can walk up stairs now." She runs up the stairs and starts bunny hopping up and down on the stage. Unfortunately her shirt is not tucked in so her bare gut is also jumping up and down. "This is what God has done for her tonight."

She's weeping. "I have four children who always had to take care of me because of the pain."

Hinn: "Now you had lupus. Tell people what that does."

"It tears the tissues of the body and makes your arthritis swell up so that you can't walk or breathe. You have to be on lots medication."

"How long have you had lupus?"

"Since I was eighteen."

"How old are you now?"

"I'm forty."

"The pain left you tonight completely?"

"Completely."

"Run!"

She awkwardly runs/bunny hops across the stage with abandon, shirt lifting, gut jumping.

I'm a bit taken by surprise when Holly says, "Okay, that just grosses me out."

I laugh. Not at the woman on the stage, but that Holly just came to the dark side a little bit.

When the lupus woman gets back to Hinn, she keeps jumping. He walks away and says to the crowd. "Somebody say Halleluiaaaaa." As he walks back toward her, two very young men in suits walk up behind her. Hinn places his hands on her forehead, and she falls back into the arms of these men who gently place her on the floor in a heap.

"God bless this woman."

"God bless this woman."

Holly quickly recovers from her grossed out state. "Okay, so the honorable thing about this is that it's not the beautiful people who he is embracing. I don't particularly want to see people like that. She's pitiful, unkempt, and unattractive. He's embracing anybody, and if anybody is accepted there, it means that I'm accepted there."

Here it has become obvious that Holly's nature leads her to look for what is honorable and good, and my nature leads me to do just the opposite.

I counter, "All the people who are the *objects* of the 'ministry' on TBN are pitiful, broke, unemployed, and/or sick and the *subjects* are healthy, perfectly groomed, and wealthy. That's how this whole thing operates. Hinn wouldn't have people who look as coiffed as himself on the stage because they clearly are not the ones who need healing."

Hinn: "Give God all the praise...."

Woman: "All the day [*sic*] of my life I give him the praise."

Hinn to the crowd: "Give her a big 'God bless you!'"

Piano music rises; crowd cheers.

This same scene plays out with a young Hispanic man with leukemia who claims that after two years of weekly blood transfusions he has been healed by attending a Benny Hinn event the night before. He screams to the crowd, "I don't need no blood, I don't need no blood!" They cheer. Hinn touches his face, and the man falls down, but not before Hinn in one smooth motion grabs the mic out of the falling man's hand.

Holly: "Boy that is rehearsed."

Wait a minute, Holly is supposed to be the one who can help me be less cynical. Uh oh. Could be some rough waters ahead.

Holly: "A cynic would say that he's making it all up and it's not spiritual at all, but is entirely a manipulation. That is one way of looking at this whole thing. On the other hand there is the fact that there are people who have this ability to sense what is happening in other people. It's not in my world, but... how horrible if he's making it all up."

Holly is struggling as hard to be innocent as I am trying to become innocent; we're just coming at it from different sides of the spectrum.

I hate to say this, but I keep thinking about an early church heresy: Donatism. The Donatists were on the scene in the fourth and fifth centuries, and their biggest issue was with priests who had abandoned the faith during Roman persecution only to come back once the dust had settled. Donatists believed that the sacraments were not efficacious if distributed by such sinful traitors. The official church doctrine that came out of this controversy and that still holds today is *ex opere operato* — from the work having been worked — in other words that the validity of sacraments depends upon the holiness of God, not the human being who distributes them, and thank goodness because there would be a hell of a lot fewer Eucharists and baptisms if this were not the case. Like zero.

So the point is that I am not a Donatist. Therefore, if the Word of God can be proclaimed in my preaching, can actually come through me, as deeply flawed as I am, then on some level I have to allow for the possibility that the healing of God can come through a charlatan like Benny Hinn. I don't *want* to admit this, but there is no other way to be consistent.

Cut to Hinn in the studio.

Hinn: "I'm asking many of you to become partners for a dollar a day to literally take the gospel to the ends of the earth, to many nations through television and crusades. We also feed children all around the world, in the Philippines, Mexico, all around the world. Over forty thousand children are being blessed by your love." Feeding hungry children is, of course, a good thing, but I don't see how what we just saw was the gospel, because doesn't Jesus have something to do with that?

Hinn (to the at-home audience): "I love you, and remember nothing is impossible with the Lord. All is well. Cast all your cares upon him; he cares for you."

Cut to an ad for his *Names of Jesus* book.

◆◆◆

Holly responds: "*We* don't have a problem taking an offering after the sermon. It supports the church and so forth and this is their offertory. If there is no opportunity for a response, then we're left without the capacity to respond to our faith. Response is a critical part of the faith. I never thought that my grandmother, who was an Oral Roberts follower, didn't have faith. She felt courage because of him; he empowered her; he fed a deep part of her. But later on when her money went to him, we her family were sorry about that."

◆◆◆

An African pastor preaches, "Though people are not around you praising you and you are seemingly walking alone, the angels of the Lord are surrounding you. In these days you are *not* alone."

Holly: "You are not alone, but people *are* so alone with their televisions. When I visit shut-ins on pastoral calls, the TV stays on. I do think that the television becomes a link with reality, if it weren't there they'd have to be out on their porches or something. It's created more isolation and then in turn it appeals to isolation."

THE ROUNDUP

Old Testament passages cited: Zero.

New Testament passages cited: Zero.

Cost of products offered: $415.
   Taking the Gospel to the ends of the earth: $360.
   Names of Jesus book: $30.
   The Name of Jesus bracelet: $25 ("it would be such a great witness
      and testimony; men and women can wear it")

Running total after 8 hours: $2038.94

Thought for this half-hour: Jesus said, "Where two or more are gathered, I'll be present." If one of them is the TV, does that still count?

The 700 Club
(Pentecostal Romper Room)
1:00 p.m.

The *700 Club* is a Christian news magazine on the air since 1966. The set is fairly indistinguishable from that of *Good Morning America* and the like. The co-anchors, Gordon and Terri, are attractive and reassuring Baby Boomers. The *700 Club*'s format is that of a straight-up news magazine, transitioning between the likable co-hosts chatting on armchairs to the "news room," where deep voiced men with strong jaws and serious faces exude authority.

The first news story, covering a drought in the American South, is followed up with comments about bizarre weather patterns in the South and wild fires in the West. A voice-over tells us, "It's time for people to wake up to what is happening and start praying." Is that a thinly veiled end-times message? At what point in history was the weather *not* bizarre? It's weather.

◆◆◆

The apocalyptic weather report is followed by "news" stories about:

+ Iran's nuclear program
+ Persecution of Christians in Palestine
+ The approval of a flag ceremony at military funerals that includes Christian language
+ Nano technology radios

◆◆◆

What makes Christian news "Christian"? Popular news themes on TBN are: signs of the end times, supporting the state of Israel, Christian persecution, and personal morality. I daydream for a few minutes about TBN founders Paul and Jan Crouch sitting in their opulent living room for twenty-four hours watching progressive Christian television (that's the first clue that this is dream and not reality — there is no such thing as progressive Christian TV, or radio or . . . well, okay, there's *Sojourner*'s magazine). Jan might turn to Paul, brushing a stray thicket of her enormous pink wig away from her face, and say, "What in the world is 'Christian' about repenting of environmental sin, aligning with the poor among us, racial equality, living simply, reconciliation, and radical hospitality?"

◆◆◆

The female host introduces a segment on racism in America: Is there a new civil rights movement? Coming up.

This should be interesting. I feel locked and loaded.

◆◆◆

Wow. Holly and I agree: the segment was really impressive. Focusing on the real difficulties in America, they touched on several perspectives concerning issues of economics, history, hate, privilege, and misunderstanding. They had interviews with not only local residents in Jena, a small southern town in the midst of a racially bifurcating legal case, but also Fox news commentator and NPR personality Juan Williams. The segment was well produced, edgy, and balanced. I don't know what to say. As a so-called "liberal," if I cannot cast my gaze upon the religious right and condemn them for being backward racists, then what am I to do? They even use *our* text: Galatians 3:26–29.

Holly: Hey, that's the progressive Christian text of choice!

Exactly. "There is no longer Jew or Greek, there is no longer slave or free, there is no longer male and female; for you are one in Christ Jesus." I'm reminded of a Simpson's episode where flamboyant film director John

Waters voices the character of a gay interior decorator who befriends Homer. When the character comes out to Homer, informing him that "it's okay that I'm queer," Homer replies, "Queer"? You can't use that word. That's *our* word to make fun of you and we neeeeed it!" So while I'm coming up short on issues to have with their treatment of race, I realize that inside I'm whining a little bit: "You can't have racial reconciliation; that's *our* issue and we neeeeed it."

♦♦♦

Holly asks, "Do you have any conservatives coming?"
"My parents are evangelicals."
"They would watch this?"
"No way."
"That's too bad."
I agree (that it's too bad I didn't get more conservative folks to join me, not that my folks don't watch TBN).

♦♦♦

My guest Mark K. George is Associate Professor of Hebrew Bible at the Iliff School of Theology in Denver. A Christian who was raised in a theologically conservative home, he teaches the Old Testament/ Hebrew Bible in a theologically progressive school, where he seeks to help students deepen their knowledge and understanding of the Bible, as well as develop robust theological understandings of it.

♦♦♦

Mark and I say farewell to Holly, and I brew a fresh pot of my new best friend. I'm kind of surprised at how energized I feel, but it's becoming a bit difficult to make myself pay attention to the TV, especially with Mark George here. I love Mark. He's about the whitest man I've ever met, kind of like if Captain America was a lapsed Presbyterian working as a Hebrew Bible scholar. He's known for claiming that God can be a bit of a tyrant in the Old Testament. A love of the biblical text runs deep in Mark, deep enough that he doesn't hold back in his engagement with it. He demands a great deal from the text, his students, and himself. Mark is married to a Jewish woman, Pam Eisenbaum, who is a New Testament scholar.

♦♦♦

The next *700 Club* segment focuses on a story about a former heroin dealer who quit dealing after having a spiritual breakdown while counting thousands of dollars of drug money.

The host then encourages those at home who are struggling with addiction or sin of any kind to pray that Jesus enters their hearts and be God for them. After the prayer he instructs us that those who believe in their hearts and confess with their mouths shall be saved.

"Confess with your mouth now. Call that toll-free number at the bottom of your screen. There will be someone on the other end to pray with you. We have a free packet with a CD teaching on how to live the Christian life."

They encourage us to get a Bible and start with the Gospel of John and to join a church, but it all starts with the phone call to that toll-free number.

Advertisement: 700 Club membership for 65 cents a day. A blindingly white Jesus carries his cross through inner city streets, Middle East markets, Asian rice paddies. "Jesus Is the Answer for the World Today" plays.

◆◆◆

We ignore the on-screen prayer while I turn to Mark and ask his response. Mark:

> I actually had to make an apology in one of my classes because I needed to be clear that I was not interested in bashing Jesus — just some theologies about Jesus. I'm interested in students having vibrant theologies that they can articulate for themselves and not simply regurgitate; theology should be vibrant and vital, not just unaware. If you say, "Jesus loves me," that's fine, but on Christian radio the other day they were hocking a book that claimed to help provide people with "Bible answers" for the Jehovah's Witnesses who come to their doors. And they claimed, "These Bible answers really boil down to 'Jesus Loves me,'" and I thought, "That's your Bible answer? That's crap."

◆◆◆

Next we get an "It happened to me" testimony from a woman who describes being diagnosed with depression after experiencing debilitating fatigue during finals week. She knew she wasn't depressed, but she still could not get out of bed. While watching the *700 Club,* Terri, the female host, had a "word of knowledge" which is the term for what I call the *Romper Room* ending to some TBN shows. *Romper Room* was a kids show that ran from the 1950s to the early 1980s. At the end of each broadcast, the hostess would look through a "magic mirror" (in reality, a face-sized open hoop with a handle) and name the children she saw in "televisionland."

She would begin with the rhyme: "Romper, bomper, stomper boo. Tell me, tell me, tell me, do. Magic mirror, tell me today. Have all my friends had fun at play?" She would then lead into "I can see Scotty and Kimberly and Julie and Jimmy and Marcie and all of you boys and girls out there!"

(Miss Jan never saw Nadia. Not once. Being a child with a Russian name during the Cold War boded poorly for one's chances of Miss Jan seeing you through her magic mirror.)

The point being that some TBN on-air personalities do this *Romper Room* thing where they basically say, "Magic mirror, tell me and say, have any of my viewers been healed today? I see someone with back problems who is now free from pain. Someone watching has a blood clot which is being thinned by God," etc.

That day apparently Terri had said "There is somebody out there who is incredibly weak with no power in her body. Lie there now and receive God's quickening power." The woman with the "it happened to me" testimony "claimed" Terri's magic mirror thing and felt energy come into her body, walked two miles that day, and passed her final.

"That's so general," Mark responds. "What are the odds that someone watching TBN during the day is a bit low on energy? Aerobics teachers aren't exactly watching the *700 Club* at 1:30 on a Friday."

"I can't really doubt her faith though," I claim. "That's what is difficult here. The *700 Club* did some good in this woman's life, yet I think they're full of hooey. Can both of those things be true?"

"There were faith healing classes at Fuller Seminary," Mark claims, "and my friend actually had her leg lengthened. She no longer walks with a limp. Can I explain that? Not really."

Me: "I'm very aware that I lose something with my cynicism. I wish I could be more like Holly and see the good but still keep a critical stance. That seems like a fuller life to me. Every program she watched she was looking for the good. I do not move through the world that way at all."

Mark: "Is a cynic a hopeful person gone bad?"

Me: "No, I'm really hopeful, or else I wouldn't be starting a church. I think I can maybe participate in God's work in the world despite my cynicism, or maybe even because of it."

Mark: "Maybe that's why we get along so well. In my lecture on David I say that I would never want to have King David over because he's as likely to plunge a dagger in my heart as sing me a song. But I still love the fact that supposedly he's the man after God's own heart."

Me: "There is hope right there."

Mark: "Indeed, but it's a perverse hope."

Me: "Perverse hope is enough for me. I find it comforting."

◆◆◆

Terri and Gordon read several letters from viewers who "claimed the healing" after Terri and Gordon offered a "word of knowledge" for their conditions.

They tell viewers to place their own hands on the area of our bodies that need healing. They pray "in agreement" and list several ailments.

"There is someone who wears a compression thing on your leg because of clots and God has just touched you and you are healed." "Someone is suffering from migraines and is now healed."

I can't help but say, "That 'agreement in prayer' thing, I think it means that if we gang up on God, then God has to do what we say." Yes, God is no match for two humans with a wish list.

◆◆◆

Advertisement: Holy Family Fabergé-style egg, $250. I'll take four.

The benefit of time has not made the egg any more tasteful. Unfortunately it's as tacky and baffling as the first time I saw it this morning.

◆◆◆

My phone rings. It's my friends Mark and Kae, the pastors at Mercy Seat in Minneapolis. They're watching the *700 Club* right now as an act of Christian solidarity with me, their fellow member in the lunatic fringe of the Lutheran Church.

Kae: "Are you touching body parts right now?"

Me: "Yes! My Hebrew Bible prof is here and we're totally touching body parts and praying . . . oh wait, that doesn't sound good at all."

Mark George interjects: "We're touching our *own* body parts."

Me: "That's not a whole lot better."

Kae and Mark are wondering how long I've been at it, and I realize it's been nine hours. How can that be true? It's going by so fast. I ask if they could maybe pitch in and get me the Fabergé-style egg for Christmas.

◆◆◆

As soon as I hang up with Mark and Kae, my friend Rachael, a brilliant Episcopalian lay woman from Minneapolis, IMs me, apparently watching as well: "Someone right now is encountering a feeling of nausea and Lord in Jesus' name she is free of that feeling, because it is now a commercial break. Praise you God, Praise."

Advertisement: Shadow of the Apocalypse, by Paul Crouch, $13.

THE ROUNDUP

Old Testament passages cited: Zero.

New Testament passages cited: Four.

Cost of products offered: $500.25

Running total after 8½ hours: $2539.19

God: Not a lot of mention.

Jesus: Even less mention.

Thought for the show: If people watching are "getting healed," then is the *700 Club* honestly doing some good in the world?

Intermission
REFLECTION ON THE BLANK SCREEN
What Are People Getting Out of This?

IN WHAT WAYS do the watching of and giving to TBN benefit those who do so? This question has plagued me throughout this entire process. I'd be wrong to say that there is no benefit whatsoever. People get something out of consuming TBN programming; if that benefit extends beyond simple entertainment, then what is its character?

I did make something of an effort to try to recruit fans of TBN to be one of my fellow viewers, but to no avail. It ends up that I don't know anyone who watches TBN. And not only that but, apparently, I don't even seem to know anyone *who knows anyone* who watches TBN. I asked around.

Any attempt on my part to try to define the benefit of something so foreign to me would be far-reaching to say the least. I'm not an academic who might have a license to do such reaching, but I do have my hunches.

It could be said that religious life is about meaning-making and an expression of social cohesion. The problem with trying to understand the sociological function of TBN for those who consume the programming is that the social function seems moot. I joked earlier. "When Jesus said, 'Where two or more are gathered, I am with you,' if one is the TV, does that count?" But there is something substantive about that question. Perhaps the *perception* of community you might have when preachers talk to you personally and when you feel as though you are "practically right there" with a TV congregation is enough to fulfill the social function of religion. Consistently the TBN on-air personalities look directly into the camera and talk "to the folks at home," creating a false intimacy between viewer and preacher. That is to say, false from my perspective, but perhaps very real from the perspective of the viewer.

❖❖❖

"Because human beings, as symbol-using creatures, cannot endure meaninglessness for long, they create meaning from the available cultural options. In modern society those options are primarily secular. Contemporary religious responses to the secularization of meaning have tended toward accommodation to, or reactionary rejection of, the surrounding dominant culture of consumption."
— Janice Peck, *The Gods of Televangelism*

John Hagee
[*again, yea!*]
(*How is a frozen pizza recall "news,"*
or "Christian," or "Christian news"?)
2:00 p.m.

After the fun of the *700 Club*, I'm struggling to give a flip about John Hagee, the hateful, jowly, state-of-Israel lovin', John McCain-endorsing, apocalyptic preacher. He's so scary, even the second time.

❖❖❖

Advertisement: Holy Land tour with John Hagee, $3,759.

Advertisement: DVD titled *Obsession: Radical Islam's War against the West*, $20. Tagline: "If you're not a radical Islamic fascist, then you need to see *Obsession.*"

❖❖❖

Hagee quotes Isaiah 62:1, 6, Genesis 12:3, Exodus 1:8 and 14, Zechariah 2, and Luke 7:1–5 during his opening statement, so I ask Mark what he thinks of this exegetical Dagwood sandwich that Hagee has just served up on the apocalyptic demand that Christians support the modern state of Israel. Mark answers:

> There is, indeed, a strain of thinking in the prophetic literature that envisions a future day when the nations (the non-Jews) will stream

to Israel and Jerusalem and worship in the temple. There even is a view that the nations/*goyim* will serve as priests in the temple. Of course, there are other, opposing, views on the matter. See Ezra and Nehemiah. The interpretive question is, which is the view to which modern readers should listen at any one time? Apocalypticism runs right through all of this. How much do we at Iliff Seminary talk about the end times? I never talk about it in Hebrew Bible class. I don't teach Daniel because I think it's loopy. And you remember me talking about Ezekiel? I want to play "Purple Haze" as an introduction to that particular prophet. Anyway, wasn't the world supposed to end at the turn of the millennium, and yet here they are talking about end times *again.*

I find Mark's cavalier attitude toward apocalypticism to be pure entertainment, and it's helping my bad attitude about having to watch Hagee again.

(Having interesting people come to my house all day to talk about religion is about the most fun thing I can think of. Which in a way is also the saddest thing I can think of. Oh well.)

◆◆◆

Advertisement: Against All Odds, video, $22

◆◆◆

CBN news story on a frozen pizza recall.

Mark: "What makes a frozen pizza recall Christian news?"

That's one of the questions of the day: What makes something "Christian"? On the one hand I hold what can be called an incarnational theology, meaning that I believe the world and everything in it is God's, that in the incarnation of Christ (the God-Man), God entered fully into the muck of our human existence. What is "spiritual" or "godly" then is not that which is not-earthly, or that which is not-physical, but just the opposite. To me, Christ is present not only in the Eucharist, in the church, and in the scriptures. Christ is also present in the suffering of the neighbor, in the least and the lame, and in every act of forgiveness. Christ is present in the dive bar down the street as much as Christ is present at the altar. On the other hand, I cringe at what some refer to as "the Christian-Industrial Complex": radio station, cable networks, music labels, T-shirt companies, and bookstores that provincially cater to the "Christian" market. What makes these shows and books and music "Christian"? Because I'm Christian, and these things tend to make *me* think that maybe perhaps there is no God after all. If reference to Christ, even in passing, is the standard for calling something Christian, then I'm not certain someone the likes of Joel Osteen or Paula White or John Hagee would qualify.

THE ROUNDUP

Old Testament passages cited: Nine, plus Book of Esther and a few chapters in Genesis

New Testament passages cited: Ten

Cost of products offered: $3,801.

Running total after 9½ hours: $6340.19

God: Sovereign, and with some pretty specific requirements of us which, if unfulfilled, will cause God to not protect us against the terrorists and thus bring down all of Western civilization and the Muslim extremists will win.

Jesus: He was a nice guy when he was here the first time but will be a bad ass the next time. Watch out.

Thought for this half-hour: Ask publisher if we might use this claim on the back cover: "If you're not a radical Islamic fascist, then you need to buy this book."

Intermission
REFLECTION ON
THE BLANK SCREEN
What Makes Something "Christian"?

S O WHY IS THE ART of Thomas Kincade, that modern-day Christian version of Bob Ross, sold in the form of paintings, calendars, and coffee mugs in so many evangelical homes? Is it simply due to the fact that he signs his paintings with John 3:16? If so, you have to give it to him, because regardless of how aesthetically questionable it may be, there is an implied righteousness to a Thomas Kincaid painting, and that righteousness is highly marketable.

I'm fairly certain that the descriptor "Christian" when applied to music and TV shows is not an indicator of theological content but instead points to what is absent: profanity, homosexuals, liberals, uncertainty — basically anything that would challenge a particular worldview. The absence of these things make a product "Christian." It certainly is not the presence of any content related to Christ per se.

So far today TBN has said precious little of Christ, perhaps a half-dozen mentions, and most of those were "calling on the name" of Jesus as talisman and did not involve the nature, work, or teachings of Christ. What seems to qualify as Christian is that which is clean, smug, overly groomed, socially conservative, and above all wrapped in super-duper positive thinking. If Jesus were here it would be hard to envision him on the set of a TBN show, except perhaps if he were turning over their Louis XVI money-changing tables.

Breakthrough with Rod Parsley
(*I wonder if "Raise eyes to heaven" was on the teleprompter?*)
2:30 p.m.

My guest Kevin R. Maly serves as Pastor of St. Paul Lutheran Church (ELCA) in downtown Denver. He holds the doctor of philosophy degree and has taught at the University of Denver; the University of Colorado, Denver; the former St. Thomas Catholic Seminary; and Regis Jesuit University, where he was also active in campus ministry and service-learning initiatives. He also served as a lobbyist and community organizer for a faith-based civil rights organization in Colorado on behalf of lesbian, gay, bisexual, and transgender people following the murder of Matthew Shepherd.

◆◆◆

Kevin arrives just in time to meet Mark George before Mark has to take his leave. Kevin is a brilliant scholar and gifted preacher, I can't wait to hear his reactions to *PTL*.

I realize that the 2:30 p.m. edition of *Breakthrough* will be identical to the 8:00 a.m. one (see page 39), except for the addition of Kevin Maly on the couch to my left. I'll spare you both my regurgitated thoughts and Rod Parsley's bloviation and instead offer you Kevin's incisive commentary, bereft of context and in its natural state:

◆◆◆

"I don't know if I even live in the same universe as this guy."

"Is this God-as-micromanager of everyone's lives?"

"I wonder if 'Raise eyes to heaven' was on the teleprompter"

"Parsley is making a pitch to help the Christian Sudanese refugees and implies that if you give money to his organization then God will give you a sevenfold blessing. So God screwed up in Sudan . . . but will do miracles in your life if you just do the right things? But if Parsley believes that people are 'blessed' if they are righteous, then by implication are the Christian Sudanese not righteous?"

"Apparently the gospel doesn't work in this particular theological system."

THE ROUNDUP

Old Testament passages cited: Three, plus his own retelling of Exodus.

New Testament passages cited: Zero.

Cost of products offered: $79.95 – $1,037.95.

Running total after 10 hours: $6420.14

God: Not mentioned too much except that God will release a sevenfold blessing to those who give money.

Jesus: Said the name once as a talisman.

Thought for this half-hour: I ❤ Kevin.

Praise the Lord (PTL)
(*Don Ho sings the bad theology of your childhood*)
3:00 p.m.

PTL is next. From what I've seen so far, I'm bracing for two hours of B-list celebrities, praise music, and gold furniture. Surely Jan Crouch will make an appearance. I'm a bit resentful of not yet having the opportunity to take in the big pink wig of holiness.

◆◆◆

What is happening? Have they preempted *PTL*? The intro for whatever show comes next is a steady stream of idealized patriotic images of Americana set to triumphal background music. The Washington Memorial, the Liberty Bell, "O! say can you see," the U.S. Constitution (the music is getting painfully operatic), "the bombs bursting in air," paintings of the Union Army, "yet wave . . ." obese white man unfurling the

flag... "of the freeeeeeeeeee," hobbled over man with cane slowly climb-
ing the steps of the Lincoln Memorial... (Oh my gosh... there's another
verse?) "And the lantern of hope..." Eisenhower, V-Day newspaper cover,
young soldier hugging a woman... (key changes to a range that has me
concerned for the ears of nearby dogs), "now we look to the skys..." cross-
topped steeple of a quaint white clapboard church, people saluting the flag
(another key change? I didn't know there was another key), firefighters
raising a flag, jets taking off from aircraft carriers, little African American girl carrying the flag in a parade, a political convention, "Land of the
freeeeeeee and the home of the braaaaave (key change). Americaaaaa (key
change), Americaaaaaaaaa (key change), Americaaaaaaa," children saluting the American and Christian flags (now we hear clapping... a studio
audience?), Timpany pounding, flags waving, audience cheering.

◆◆◆

Kevin: "This is idolatry, pure and simple."

◆◆◆

(Announcer) "From Coast to coast and around the world it's time to
praise the Lord.... It's a special military testimony night."
     Paul Crouch Jr. is hosting. The largely military audience stands and
cheers.
     PC Jr.: "In reality it is me who should be giving you a standing ovation
right now."
     Kevin: "Can you say 'pandering'?"
     PC Jr. introduces his father and the founder of TBN, Paul Crouch, as a
guest. Inviting an army chaplain up to the stage, Crouch gushes over how
this man has blessed him. He has given him the army issue Bible, an NIV
version (of course), covered in army camo. Crouch asks if he could read a
scripture "for all you precious ones who have made TBN the great voice
that it is around the world, over twelve thousand outlets now worldwide.
There's hardly a spot left on earth; the devil can't hide anywhere now."
They read Psalm 68:11: " 'The Lord gave the word, great was the company
of those who published it.' That is our TBN family."
     Paul holds up a letter and begins:

This arrived yesterday. "Hello, a friend told me that you have special
information for Muslims, I am a Muslim. My friend told me that
Jesus is #1. How do I find him? Thank you for true information —
Hussain." They are hungry. Let's just pray. Take the hand of someone

next to you. [Kevin shoots me a look that says, "Try to take my hand and it's all over between us."]

Crouch takes the chaplain's hand, the camera focusing in on their clasped hands.

Father, we lift our hearts in love and admiration to you, knowing that this is *your* work. Man has not done this; this has been your work. We give you praise and honor and glory. We bow at your footstool to give you the praise of our hearts. Thank you for Jesus, for his blood, and for the comfort of the Holy Spirit. Let this be a night of praise and worship that would lift Jesus ever higher. That the world may see his beauty and be drawn to the Prince of Peace.

It's interesting that they choose to begin their night of honoring the military by first honoring themselves and the "great" work of TBN. Crouch has opened with a prayer that "this night might help the world see Jesus' beauty and be drawn to the prince of peace." I'll take that as the measure by which the next two hours should be judged. Game on.

♦♦♦

They cut to a segment given to them by ABC News: "Welcome Home a Hero." For three hundred days of the last year Burt Brady, a sixty-nine-year-old vet, has gone out to the Dallas–Fort Worth airport to cheer on, hug, and welcome home the soldiers. He's joined by students, homemakers, retirees — and Vietnam and Korean war vets who themselves did not receive a warm welcome home, but quite the opposite. The soldiers coming off the tarmacs choke up with gratitude. I'm actually a little choked up myself.

That is undeniably a beautiful act of love.

Despite my liberal credentials, I am a military brat who still has a great deal of respect for those who serve in the military. My father enlisted in the Air Force at age eighteen and at twenty-eight became an officer. Then after doctoral work, he served on the faculty of the Air Force Academy, a fact of which I am very proud. To this day, when I see even a film clip of the U.S. Air Force Thunderbirds fly over I tear up. I cannot talk smack about people who serve in the military. To see the story about this man who pours himself out to show love to these young kids coming back from the horrors of war is very gospel to me.

PC Jr. interviews Bob Weiland, a Vietnam veteran who lost his legs in that war and is now an inspirational speaker. "Energetic" doesn't begin to describe this guy.

PC Jr.: "You didn't let losing your legs send you into depression?"

Weiland: "I cast all my cares upon Him. But legs are cool, man. I don't care what anyone says. I don't want to give you the wrong impression. But we learn to rely on our heavenly Father, Jesus Christ." (All those in attendance at the council of Nicea are now rolling in their graves.)

PC Jr.: "How were you treated when you got home?"

Wieland: "Why be a complainer? Let's come up with a solution. Tonight is part of that; let's keep it going."

Kevin's response is searing. "When you honor all the people who have served, it distracts from asking what the hell was happening in the first place that they had to become canon fodder. Who is it serving anyway? The powerful, the elite, the privileged."

Verne Jackson, a man who must be in his seventies wearing a leather blazer and a stars and stripes tie, sings "This Is My Country."

Me: "I never thought I'd say this, but now I wish it actually was a praise song."

Kevin: "Isn't it though? It's a hegemonic discourse: assent of the oppressed by raising an ideological superstructure. What better than *God and country?*"

This is why I love Kevin; he not only says things like "hegemonic discourse" and "ideological superstructure," but he actually knows what they mean. I see his point. I'm reminded of when my friend Sean was doing stand-up during the first Gulf War. He would say, "I find myself being in the unenviable position of being *for* the war, yet *against* the troops." Yeah, that's gotta suck.

Dressed in full military dress, the next guest, Army chaplain Etterbeek, describes his deployment in Iraq and the biblical sites he encountered, namely, the fiery furnace that Shadrach, Meshach, and Abednego endured in the book of Daniel. It is a fire pit in the desert, a fire he claims has never gone out. They show a short clip in which an American soldier, huge gun in hand, stands beside a large patch of sand that is on fire. I guess I always thought that the furnace in Joshua was more of, I don't know, a furnace I guess.

PC Jr.: "Tell us what TBN is doing over there." (Seriously? This self-authentication is wearing me down.)

Chaplain: "The Iraqis didn't have satellite dishes. It was all propaganda done by Saddam, so they didn't trust anything on the radio or TV. Then when Dr. Crouch came over and started making those satellite dishes available, it opened up a whole new world for them. There are Christians in Iraq, and it gave them some resources to connect with the Universal Christian church all over the world."

PC Jr.: "You know those of you who love and support TBN, you know Dad took that scripture literally that said, 'Go into all the world and preach the gospel' — and that is exactly what we're doing. We have an Arabic channel, a Farsi channel. There is literally no place on earth except Antarctica where you cannot receive TBN. A few penguins may not get saved, but that's okay."

I think I just threw up a little bit.

A taped segment on the Medal of Honor recipients follows. I find Medal of Honor recipients to be mesmerizing. I've seen these interviews before, and they tell amazing stories of selflessness and courage. These are noble men who express the honor of wearing a medal that represents those who achieved more than they did, but for whom no witnesses were living. "This medal is not mine; it belongs to all those kids who never grew up to be grandfathers. I just hold it in trust."

Kevin: "This is hagiography."

I suppose, in what my husband calls "the folk religion of God Bless America," Medal of Honor films are the closest thing to hagiography we've got.

◆◆◆

"I wonder how they'd react to this Sunday's readings?" Kevin asks before leaving.

I'm not preaching Sunday and am ignorant of what the lectionary readings are. As Kevin gets ready to leave, I look it up:

> But I say to you that listen, Love your enemies, do good to those who hate you, bless those who curse you, pray for those who abuse you. If anyone strikes you on the cheek, offer the other also; and from anyone who takes away your coat do not withhold even your shirt. Give to everyone who begs from you; and if anyone takes away your goods, do not ask for them again. Do to others as you would have them do to you. (Luke 6:27–31)

How ironic.

◆◆◆

My guest Sara Pierce: Born October 7, 1978, to Jim and Cay Pierce (now blissfully divorced). I was going to be named Emily until my mother saw my premature little face and realized that Sara was more appropriate. I was brought up in the Lutheran Church alongside my older sister, Rachel, and my younger sister, Abby. We attended Sunday school every Sunday and soon realized that the answer was always "Jesus." I belonged to the local Youth for Christ organization in junior high and high school and attended Wartburg College (a private Lutheran school), where I received my bachelor's degree in religion. Since then I have done two years in the Urban Servant Corps and have attended St. Paul's Lutheran Church in Denver and St. Matthew's Lutheran Church in Aurora. I consider myself a Christian, believing in Christ as a person and a teacher and believing that Christianity is very personal to each and every person who practices it.

◆◆◆

"Kevin said that this is just simply idolatry: worshiping the symbols of the country," I tell Sara and Neil. "I think when they talk about our freedom and how great America is, they are really talking about our standard of living: the fact that we all have cars and can choose between forty-three different brands of potato chips."

Sara begins to talk about her experiences in different churches: "I was involved in a Harvest church once, and they would tell you before leaving that they were going to ask you the next week how many people you saved."

Me: "Like Shaklee?"

Sara: "Yep. Then I was involved in a more Covenant type church, which was all about the 'love the sinner hate the sin' thing with gays. Come to think of it, they were a bit like Village of the Damned. That was fine and good until I got out into the world and started to form relationships with people in the gay community. Then it was like 'Wait a minute, they're not sinners.' Then I had to leave."

◆◆◆

Brian Fleming, Purple Heart recipient, comes on screen. He's also in his military uniform, but he looks like he's about fifteen years old. He tells of his vehicle in Afghanistan being blown up by an IED. Saying that prayer is what saved him, he tells how God answers prayer, because his wife and mother were praying fervently for his return, and here he is. This, of course, begs the question. "Do the wives and mothers and husbands and fathers of those who have died in our current wars not pray hard enough?" What must people who are mourning the deaths of their loved ones be feeling about this particular line of theological thought?

Brian: "To everyone who has prayed even once for our soldiers, thank you because I am here today because of that" [and those other guys would not have died had you prayed harder, prayed more, prayed better?].

PC Jr.: "You know, continue to pray for Brian as he'll be leaving the Army shortly, but he'll be a soldier in the Army of God."

I'm having a flashback to my Church of Christ childhood. Songs with titles like "Soldiers of Christ, Arise," "Faith Is the Victory," "I'm in the Lord's Army," "Onward, Christian Soldiers," "Stand Up, Stand Up for Jesus (ye soldiers of the cross)" are ringing through my head. I've always wanted someone to do a three-CD set of gospel music. The first would be all soldier-battle-war songs, the second would be all about the gold and jewels we get in heaven ("I've Got a Mansion Just Over the Hilltop"), and the third? Blood . . . all about blood ("Are You Washed in the Blood?" "Power in the Blood," "Nothing but the Blood"). If Don Ho wasn't dead, I'd go for a title like *Don Ho Sings the Bad Theology of Your Childhood.* Something like that.

Mental faculties slipping . . . at eleven hours. Must brew and drink more coffee.

◆◆◆

My guest Celia Myers studied social welfare at UC Berkeley and is currently serving a year with the Urban Servant Corps in Denver. She was baptized and confirmed in an ELCA church in Southern California and still has Lutheran tendencies.

◆◆◆

Sara asks, "What do they say about PTSD and depression and the challenges these guys are going to be facing when they get home? What about that?"

◆◆◆

Celia, a young Urban Servant Corps volunteer, has just joined us for military testimony night on *PTL.* (USC is a domestic Peace Corps–type program in Denver.) Her first observation is a doozey: "The evangelicals have the tendency to interpret scriptures literally for their own agenda and then ignore other scriptures. In the same way, here they are choosing to interview only those with superstrong faith and ignore the other stories. They hold this up and say, 'Here's the truth.'"

Celia's got a point, but the truth is that we all do this. I choose to focus on the parts of the Bible that uphold my theology and ignore the parts that don't.

◆◆◆

Verne Jackson again, still with the leather blazer, breaks into "God Bless the USA." I mute the TV, which feels a little like cheating, but still, I do it for Verne.

The next *PTL* guest, Dave Roever, is also a Purple Heart recipient, only he didn't receive his metals until thirty-four years after the fact. This Vietnam vet was actually listed as dead until he convinced them otherwise. He was severely burned and even tells a humorous story about preaching at a revival in Honduras when his prosthetic ear fell off. This guy is hysterical, soooo funny and down-homey. Despite his talk about "getting people saved," I could become very fond of him.

"I never asked, 'Why, God?' I think because I didn't want to know the answer. What's he gonna say? 'I don't know Dave, there's just something about you I don't like.'"

Roever looks into the camera to beseech the audience to let Jesus into their hearts. At which point things in my living room get a bit irreverent.

Me: "This is boring."

Sara: "Your ear fell off. We get it. Next! I mean, should I be feeling bad right now because I'm not filled to the brim with faith and happiness — *and* I have both my ears?"

"Well, Sara, we *do* have some matches." Matthew offers.

Sara now feels compelled to pray the sinners prayer and calls in, but "All the prayer partners are busy, but God bless you."

◆◆◆

We're all going to hell.

THE ROUNDUP

Cost of products offered: $250 Fabergé-style egg. I'll take five.

Running total after 10½ hours: $6670.14

Thought for these two hours: God *has* blessed America. Let's start praying for God to bless Darfur and Iran and Haiti.

Intermission

REFLECTION ON
THE BLANK SCREEN
Prayer

To everyone who has prayed even once for our soldiers, thank you
because I am here today because of that.   — Soldier on *PTL*

I N THE DAYS AFTER THE BROADCAST, I showed a tape of *PTL*'s "military
testimony night" to a friend of mine who happens to be a graduate
of the Air Force Academy and is currently in seminary studying to be a
military chaplain. I was hoping she would offer insight into the Christian-
military ethos, but she had only one reaction. It was a strong one.

"I guess I just wonder" she said, "about the message that those who
survive IED explosions and gunfire do so because people at home pray for
them. If we draw clear connections between safety and prayers for safety,
then what about the prayers of families whose loved ones didn't survive?
Are we telling the families of those who die that they didn't pray well
enough or hard enough? Prayer is powerful, but complicated."

Ancient Secrets of the Bible
(CorningWare is ruined for me)
5:00 p.m.

My guest Jennifer Hampton was born in Tucson, Arizona, in 1976.
Her religious background is Christian, specifically Baptist. She, along
with her family (minus her dad), attended Baptist services until she
was thirteen, when they stopped going to church. Her extended family is very spiritual. Jennifer earned a bachelor's degree in cultural
anthropology (the profession with the highest degree of atheism),
is a lesbian, works as a sexuality educator, and usually believes in
a Higher Power, although her beliefs do not fully align with any
religious doctrine.

◆◆◆

My guest Janet Loo was born in Brooklyn, New York, in 1968. Her
religious background is Catholic. She is the youngest of five siblings
who all went to Catholic school, except for her. She did, however,

attend religious services sporadically until she was about ten. She is lesbian, and although she identifies herself as spiritual, she does not prescribe to any specific religious beliefs. Janet is a professional photographer and shot the cover of this book.

◆◆◆

Today's episode: "The Fiery Furnace: Could Anyone Survive It?"

We intro with a montage of low-budget Bible reenactments that make Charlton Heston's *Ten Commandments* look positively CGI. There's Noah with a big fluffy fake beard releasing a dove, Lot's wife turning into a pillar of homemade special-effect white-out, and Sampson knocking down spray-painted Styrofoam pillars. The show consists of events in the Bible being reenacted and then scientifically "proven" by a slate of "scholars." I'm delighted. It goes without saying that the integrity of scientific inquiry based on a conviction that the issue in question is undoubtedly fact because *God said it and now we just have to prove it* is a soaring monument to inductive reasoning.

If matters of faith need to be scientifically proven, then I have no idea what faith means to these people. Do *I* think that Shadrach, Meshach, and Abednego were literally thrown into a furnace and literally walked out without a mark on them? Is it fact? Maybe, maybe not; it makes no difference to me. Is it true? Yes, it's absolutely true. This is faith we are talking about, not biology class. Trying to prove scientifically the historical accuracy of events in the Bible is to faith what having your spouse under twenty-four-hour video surveillance is to marital trust.

It would appear that the main way in which my faith is involved in the *Ancient Secrets of the Bible* is in the suspension of disbelief it takes to accept that this type of thing ever gets made at all.

How I imagine the production meeting: "As you can see, we propose that we make a biblical reenactment show sprinkled with scholarly comments by experts. We can easily prove that the Bible is true by just acting it out and hiring some, um, 'available' Ph.D.s to say, 'Yeah, that happened.' We don't even need to indicate what school they are from; just put 'expert' below their name. The fifth-grade Sunday school class at my church is up for making the costumes and sets, so that's a win-win, and we'll get volunteers to do the acting. It's a slam dunk!"

My friend Janet, whom I've known for eighteen years, and her partner, Jennifer, whom I've just met, are here. Neither one is particularly Christian.

Realizing that I've forgotten to celebrate my halfway mark, I hook up the girls with wine, beer, or juice as the case may be and we clink glasses in celebration. My TV viewing has gone by quickly enough, but the idea of twelve more hours makes me a little queasy.

Given the "fiery furnace" film clip during the *PTL* military testimony hour, which showed a patch of continually burning ground from modern-day Iraq, I'm curious how they are going to portray the furnace.

To explore the construction of the Babylonian furnace, an expert from the Corning Company is called upon. They claim he built two similar furnaces, though why an industry-leading glass and ceramic company wants to burn Hebrew children is beyond me. He describes how furnaces can have uneven heat — creating cold spots where someone could potentially survive.

"Apply this cold spot idea to the large Babylonian furnace, and the biblical trio, with or without the help of an angel, could have survived the fiery furnace due to a set of miraculous circumstances just as the Bible describes," he tells us.

Jennifer: "I'm confused about what this is. This guy is an expert who's trying to prove they could survive a furnace?"

I take a shot. "From what I can tell, the Corning guy just said that there is a scientific explanation for how they could survive with or without an angel's help. But why then does he say that they survived due to a miracle *just as the Bible says?*" Isn't it counter-intuitive to say that a miracle is something you can prove to be scientifically possible?

◆◆◆

"Here's the deal," Jennifer offers, "Religion has benefited people all around the world, but for people who are not in it, it's hard not to see it as just oppressive and detrimental to your life, like if you're gay, for instance. This seems like a real Old Testament God thing and not a Jesus thing. It feels like maybe it's a control mechanism that historically has really functioned to keep people in line in a very specific way."

"Like keeping you from being a lesbian, for instance. That didn't work out so well, huh? They're obviously going to need to start trying a whole lot harder, their success rate is lousy."

THE ROUNDUP
Cost of products offered: Free.

Running total after 12½ hours: $6670.14

God: His miracles are just science. Just ask the Corning company.

Rediscovering the Kingdom
with Dr. Myles Munroe
(Religion as government)
5:30 p.m.

I've been through enough of these shows to have some well-honed skepticism about the title of "Doctor" among this crowd, and "Dr." Myles Munroe, our host for the next half-hour, does not get a pass. A quick Google check confirms my suspicions. Mr. Munroe is the proud owner of an honorary doctorate from Oral Roberts University.

The opening of *Rediscovering the Kingdom* is very "newsy": a spinning globe, serious music, a royal crown at the globe's center. The set is also very "news roomy." Munroe stands between a large screen and a production room with consoles, busy people, and numerous TV screens. He and his expensive suit are both very authoritative.

Janet: "What's this guy's deal? Is he a preacher or a newscaster?"

Munroe starts with the claim that people are all looking for the power to control circumstances. And that the kingdom of God restores this power Adam lost. A kingdom is not a religion but a government. Today he is focusing on ambassadors in the kingdom — rediscovering the original role and assignment of the church.

Monroe's argument is difficult to follow, but here's the best I can manage: God's plan was for his government on earth to be ruled by God through men. Man is created as God's governmental representative on earth. We are the ambassadors of God's kingdom government. The church, then, is not a religious organization, but a government office. Jesus came to establish the agency of the church to serve as ambassadors to represent the kingdom of God and to recruit citizens. God's purpose was for each person to be a king and a priest and for the Bible to be our country's constitution.

Dr. Munroe: "If someone asks you what you think about adultery or homosexuality, you say, 'As an ambassador I have no opinion about this matter, but [pointing to the Bible] my government's position is that it's an abomination.' If you have a problem with an ambassador's statement, you cannot take it up with him; you have to take it up with the government. That's why an ambassador has diplomatic immunity."

Our heads are spinning. Each of the convoluted points in his argument is being backed up by random Bible verses. Just in the last five minutes we've had: Ephesians 3:10, Isaiah 9:6, 1 Peter 2:10, Revelation 5:9–11, Ephesians 6:19–21, Ephesians 2:19, Matthew 6:24–25, Matthew 11: 27–28, Matthew 26:52, Genesis 1:26, John 15:15–16, John 16:14–15, and John 20:21–24.

This makes Jennifer rightly ask, "If you have one of these shows can you pretty much say what you want and just throw in some Bible verses to back it up?"

Dr. Munroe: "A government provides ambassadors with cars and a chauffer . . . groceries . . . pays all their bills . . . shoes for their children. That's why Jesus says do not worry what you will eat and what you will drink. You are an ambassador; all your life is heaven's responsibility, and that's why you can live free from worry and stress. If you are a religious person you have to worry, but if you are an ambassador your freedom is in the fact that the government is responsible for your life and that is the good news."

♦♦♦

I feel like I'm drowning. I just can't endure it. If the hellfire and brimstone preachers of the past tried to make us feel bad about ourselves, then these guys on TBN offer a steady stream of triumphal crapola: the whole world is there for your taking and God wants you to have every bit of it. I'm trying to imagine a world where everyone is a king and a priest and the Bible is the ruling constitution. What would this biblicist world look like? Only nuclear holocaust is coming to mind — like the entire world is in a celebrity death match in clothing without mixed fibers. In such an everyone-is-king world, who would be those chauffeurs we are promised?

THE ROUNDUP

Old Testament passages cited: Zero.

New Testament passages cited: Twenty-two.

Cost of products offered: $259.95.
  Books: *Rediscovering the Kingdom, Kingdom Principles,*
    The Most Important Person on Earth: $19.99 each.
  Rediscovering the Kingdom: DVD or CD: $99.99.

Running total after 13 hours: $6930.09

God: God is the king who gave us the Bible as his government's constitution.

Jesus: Jesus was sent to set up God's government offices.

Thought for this half-hour: Where's *my* chauffeur?

Behind the Scenes

(I think all this anointing has just given me the runs)

6:00 p.m.

My guest Dick Bolz has been married to his high school sweetheart for forty-six years. They have three children, Nadia, Gary, and Barbara. He served in the United States Air Force for over twenty-four years and later was an independent consultant to aerospace and database communities. He has served as a deacon and elder in the Church of Christ and is a self-proclaimed Zionist.

◆◆◆

My guest Peggy Newsom Bolz: I am the proud mother of Nadia Bolz-Weber. I was raised in a loving Bible-believing home that valued the scriptures and taught me to have a faith in God and his Son. My first twelve years were in a sweet-coal mining town and then in Detroit, where I attended another Church of Christ in which most members were from the South. I was baptized on January 13, 1957, at the age of thirteen. From my earliest memory I have prayed every day and had a firm belief in the power of prayer. I have been richly blessed in my sixty-five years of life and am grateful for God's grace.

◆◆◆

The opening montage is of a blue globe circling a banner of international flags. This is a "TBN international report."

My parents are here. They are faithful evangelical Christians who are still members of the Church of Christ, and although their current church would be considered "evangelical," the Church of Christ that I was raised in would easily be categorized as "fundamentalist." I'm nervous about watching this with my parents, and that perhaps may be why I am about to excuse myself and go take a shower.

Gray-haired TBN founder Paul Crouch, donning black shirt and black tie, is behind a Plexiglas pulpit with about two hundred people sitting behind him stadium style — mostly overweight women in their fifties and sixties singing "alleluia" over and over. This is the same tune we sang growing up, and my mom is singing along, maybe because Paul Crouch just told us at home to do so. This is the first (and will be the only) congregational-type singing I've seen today on TBN, and it is bringing back memories of my childhood in the Church of Christ, where the singing was in glorious four-part a capella. (Having been raised in a church with such a strong singing tradition, I was devastated by Lutheran singing, which usually feels like everyone's concentrating on making a tiny little sound designed to project from their month to the front of their hymnal and then fall immediately to the floor before being heard by anyone else).

I feel uncomfortable as hell. This song they are singing is more reminiscent of my Church of Christ upbringing than anything else I've seen on TBN, and I can't believe it's during the hour my parents are here. Outside of the singing and people who loved me, I don't have a lot of good things to say about my life in the Church of Christ, and here I am sitting with my parents watching Paul Crouch tell us to sing along. Do I roll my eyes and make a biting comment about the TBN audience and set design, or do I give in and sing the last refrain with my mom? Answer: I get up and take a shower.

After thirteen hours I'm needing to refresh a bit, helped greatly by the fact that all the "anointing with the Holy Spirit" has created a film of righteousness on my skin, which I am now compelled to exfoliate. But first I make a crack about how if TBN ever goes under they would take the Plexiglas industry with them. To which my dad comments, "The pulpits are transparent, and they can't hide behind anything." Nuts. There's a sound theological reason for Plexiglas? The shower can't come fast enough.

Paul Crouch introduces the others standing with him and then says, "We have just partaken of Holy Communion together." What? The shower can wait. This is absolutely the first mention of what would be called a sacrament. I'm wondering why there is nothing sacramental on TBN. What does communion look like in the TBN studio? Is it matzah bread and grape juice (likely) or a loaf of whole wheat and Mogen David (overwhelmingly less likely)? Do they say the words of institution or do they make up an on-the-spot prayer? I'm feeling a bit cheated here in regards to my imminent shower. In the absence of details, I wish he hadn't said anything at all so I wouldn't be totally distracted now. It's amazing to me how one thing that almost all Christians share, namely, communion, can so often separate us. The church I was raised in thought of communion as the Lord's Supper, a memorial meal, during which we were to think of Jesus' suffering and how it was caused by our sins. The matzah and juice was in no way the body and blood of Christ. In the Lutheran Church the bread and wine are the real presence of Christ. The Eucharist is a gift of God's own self and freely given to all so that we may go out fed and nourished by God's grace. I will get no clarity on the matter here.

He mentions "we have just partaken of Holy Communion," and then he mentions nothing more about it.

Paul is now talking about how he and Jan have been away for three months, "remaking the Holy Land Experience." Huh? Surely they didn't take their faux Louis XVI gold furniture and fake ferns down to spruce up the Wailing Wall—like *Prosperity Gospel Queer Eye for the Holy Land.* I'm not too sure what that means until I remember that he's talking about a new Orlando theme park that TBN owns. Or, as he says, "which God has given us. I hope you can all go down and see the wondrous works that God has done there. What makes me so excited is that sinners come through those gates every day and are exposed to the wonderful works of the Lord. The temple of Solomon has been rebuilt there."

To which my dad says, "So God wouldn't allow a man after his own heart to build the Temple but he allows Paul Crouch to build one in an amusement park?" Point for Dad. Still photos from the Holy Land Experience are shown, one of a Fabio-Jesus on stage with a boom mic and the other of the Holy of Holies complete with the ark of the covenant.

They are apparently getting ready for a telethon. They call it "passing the hat." PC Jr. and his dad banter a bit about how wonderful it is that TBN "doesn't show commercials" and instead shows "inspirational nuggets about what Jesus is doing and can do," which makes me wonder in what way is a $250 Holy Family Fabergé-style egg, the likes of which Liberace would find gaudy, something that *Jesus* is doing? Paul then reads a letter and, just like during *PTL* earlier in the day, the message is from a Muslim looking for information on Jesus. In this case the writer is in Hot Springs, North Dakota. "Hello, a friend says you have special information for Muslims. I am Muslim. My friend tells me that Jesus is number one. How do I find him? Thank you for the true information. Thanks—Hassan."

This letter mirrors that of the one read aloud on the 3:00 p.m. *Behind the Scenes* and is perhaps a standard practice for this show: read a letter from a member of the ideological "other" who has become an ideological "us" through watching TBN. Crouch continues by telling those who are watching overseas that "we love you and want to hear from you." I'm fairly convinced that during the Cold War these letters were from godless communists who were thanking TBN for bringing truth. Now they are from today's commies, the Muslims.

Paul Crouch introduces a woman in a long blue jacket who appears to be in her sixties. Her name is Aquilla Nash, and Paul calls her a "true prophetess of the Lord," who has told him many things in the spirit that have come to pass "precisely as the Lord spoke it to her." It looks as if she may have been a school nurse or perhaps a spokeswoman on one of those World War II personal hygiene public service films before becoming a "prophetess." (Note to self: What's the starting salary of a prophetess? Are there health benefits? A union? Maybe I could get in on that action.) Aquilla was set up by Jan and Paul to do a prophesy show on another network.

She reads letters from women in Muslim countries who thank TBN for bringing them the news of Jesus; they ask Aquilla to send their love to Dr. Crouch and Pastor Benny Hinn, which leads Aquilla to gush even more over Paul Crouch with praise for "all the things TBN does to get the gospel out. God uses people to raise up a voice in this hour, and all the great TBN programs that go out are made possible by the viewers."

Back to the television audience with everyone clapping. "Praise the Lord," Paul Crouch says, and then asks everyone to stand and "lift our hands in praise to the Lord and say, 'Thank you, Jesus' for this great voice. Only God could have done this. Lord, we just praise you. Praise him out loud. We give you the glory, we give you the honor."

I'm thinking, "... and the tacky ornate furniture too? Do we give Jesus the Plexiglas and the Fabergé-style eggs and polyester pantsuits and the Crouch's corporate jet?" I'm thinking Jesus might say, "Thanks but no thanks."

Paul calls a pastor up to the stage. Apparently the African American man in a clerical collar and pectoral cross leads worship at a TBN chapel at 11:00 a.m. every Sunday. He is handing Paul a vial of "Holy Land anointing oil." (It's unclear if it is from the actual Holy Land or the newly "spruced up" Holy Land in Orlando.) I can't wait to see where this is going, and I don't have to wait long for the big payoff. They are going to use the Holy Land anointing oil on the 240 telephones for the "Praise-a-thon" (TBN's big fundraising event). The studio audience is asked to lay hands on the telephones. My parents are actually squirming now.

"Lay hands on the telephones?" My dad protests. "Hard to find biblical evidence of laying hands on *anything* other than humans." There are times when my parents' biblicism is hard to take, and there are other times when it makes me want to high five them.

The audience now begins "anointing" the TBN phone bank. Paul exhorts them to "pray hard that the Lord will not only meet the financial need — he has already done that — but that he will give us precious, precious souls and that many will meet Christ during our Praise-a-thon."

He hands the mic to Aquilla as the camera pans to the audience duti-
fully coming down the aisle and dipping their fingers in the Holy Orlando
theme park oil.

Aquilla says that "there is another precious little word he dropped in
my spirit recently that he had never told me before: that he is getting
ready to parade his church, to display his church that all will see the glory
upon my people." When she says this the camera pans back to the stream
of women coming down the stairs to dip their fingers in the oil. Seriously.

They cut to the audience in the phone bank "anointing" each phone
and computer screen. Aquilla exhorts the viewing audience to "support
TBN, pray for TBN, and stand behind it because of their voice and their
ability to hear what God wants and what God is saying. I know because
they called upon me to have a program on the Church channel, and only
God could have spoken that to them. Because of their obedience I am
able to let my voice go to the nations now. Jesus said to go into the whole
world, and I know Jan and Paul's heart is to get the gospel to the ends of
the world, their heart is to see multitudes saved."

There is more phone bank anointing, and I'm thinking that my "heart
is to" have better grammar on Christian television. Aquilla continues.
"This is the best place you can put your dollar or pennies or thousands.
There is no other place I know that is more rewarding than right here
at this network. As you sow into this great network, it will come back to
you pressed down, shaken together, and flowing over. I sowed a generous
significant gift, and that is why I get to do what I get to do today."

Aquilla turns to Paul: "Don't you think that you can sow a gift literally
expecting the Lord to bring a reward?"

Paul answers, "You know I asked the Lord about that because there was
a lot of controversy a number of years ago. 'Lord, can I bring you a gift
fully expecting an answer from you for a need I might have?' Now you
can't buy a miracle from God, and you can't buy a blessing, but the Lord
said very clearly to me, 'Did I give my best gift, my only begotten son,
expecting *nothing?*' "

Paul answers God's question: "He expected *more sons and daughters.*
That's what he needed. He sowed his son — *what he needed* — and what
has he received? Thousands and millions of sons and daughters and you
and I are a part of that."

In all my years of studying theology and Bible, including atonement
theories and justification, I have never heard this. I want to be outraged,
but I'm actually pondering that idea. God gave the gift of God's son so that

God might have many more sons and daughters. God sowed what God needed. That's an interesting perspective. Then I snap out of it. "Hey, Dad, if Matthew and I want another child, which of the two we already have should we snuff out? Or maybe we could put the cat to sleep so that we might get two in return. This is chain letter theology."

To which my father replies, "I was almost disappointed in not getting the prosperity gospel message until I heard that."

I have nothing more to add and the Thai food take-out just got here.

THE ROUNDUP

Old Testament passages cited: Zero.

New Testament passages cited: Zero.

Cost of products offered: As much as you're willing and able to give.

Running total after 13½ hours: $6930.09

God: In order for God to get more sons and daughters, he sacrificed the one he had — like a cosmic chain letter. He had to do this within forty-eight hours or else the magic would not work.

Intermission
REFLECTION ON THE BLANK SCREEN
Christology, Pneumatology, and the Absence of Language

WHILE WRITING THE BOOK over the past five months, I've found myself questioning several aspects of my own Lutheran tradition, but not in a "Wow, we really got that one wrong" sort of way. It's more that by being immersed in TBN, such a different form of Christianity, I have seen where we as Lutherans are a bit weak. It's not just my experience of the book, but the experience that has paralleled it: that of establishing a new Christian community. Here's the rub: Lutherans have what is considered to be a "high Christology." In other words we think quite a lot of Jesus, namely, that he is God incarnate and not just a really great guy who got a bum rap. But I now realize we have a really low Pneumatology, that is to say, we don't talk a whole lot about the Holy Spirit. I'm certain some really hard-core Lutheran will read this and protest that Luther did indeed write about the Holy Spirit in some Reformation document in the sixteenth century, proving we do have a doctrine of the Holy Spirit. But functionally I've heard precious little Holy Spirit discourse in my Lutheran circles. Of course, many other traditions, including some represented on TBN, have high Pneumatologies. They are all about the Spirit (and not so much about Jesus); that's where I think all the "anointing" language comes in.

I have been overwhelmed by my experience of being a "church planter." (I hate that term, but I also hate gardening, so the two may very well be related.) The grace, serendipity, "coincidence," and blessing we've all experienced over the past ten months have been extraordinary, making our community feel as though the Spirit is at work. Our efforts alone could never have created what House for All Sinners and Saints has become in this short time. Acknowledging this presents two challenges for me:

1. I have almost no language to talk about this experience. My Lutheran tradition has failed me on this. We're so terrified of anything smacking of emotionalism or sounding like "those people" (Pentecostals, evangelicals, charismatics), that we have stepped away from having a rich vocabulary for how the Spirit does indeed move in our lives and in our communities. I can't bear saying that "I feel the anointing of the Holy Spirit," but I also can't deny that I think this might actually be what we're experiencing.

2. In talking about the beauty of this new community — how so many people keep coming out of the woodwork to be a part of us, how healing it is for people who have been rejected by the church to be welcomed into Christian community again — seeing tears stream down the faces of my friends during liturgy, I say, "This is God's work, not ours." The problem is that Paul Crouch said these exact words during *Behind the Scenes* at TBN when he talked about how much TBN has grown, how it's taking the gospel to the ends of the earth, and how so many people's lives have been changed because of it: "This is God's work, not ours."

What if we are both right? Part of me can't bear the thought, but what if it's true? In the book of Genesis God blessed both Sarah and Hagar, so maybe God blesses and, despite the lousy raw material God has to work with, manages still to get something done through both our community and (*gasp*) TBN.

The Hal Lindsey Report
(Meet my dad)
6:30 p.m.

Hi there. This is Nadia's dad. Nadia is taking a much-needed break and will be back after a refreshing shower and a bite to eat. Until then, you'll need to suffer with me for a bit.

I think it fair to give you a filter whereby you can evaluate my words. I am a Christian and an unabashed Zionist according to Webster (a member of a movement formerly for reestablishing and now for supporting the Jewish national state of Israel). I also served twenty-four years in the U.S. military. I energetically supported the action in Afghanistan and, with equal energy, opposed and continue to oppose the action in Iraq.

In the 1970s I was one of nearly 9 million people who read *The Late, Great Planet Earth* by Hal Lindsey. I was captivated by the book but not frightened. Regarding end-times theology I am *not* a premillennialist nor a postmillennialist nor an amillennialist. I guess I am, as a man recently stated, a panmillennialist. I believe that everything is going to pan out. Now, on to the show.

Mr. Lindsey warns us appropriately about the dangerous president of Iran, Mahmoud Ahmadinejad. He begins the segment with the following words:

> It should be painfully obvious that Washington is even more serious about this nuclear program than it was about Saddam Hussein. We strongly suspected that Saddam had nuclear devices or was trying to acquire them. . . . In Iran's case there is absolutely no doubt of either Iran's nuclear program or Ahmadinejad's intended purpose for it.

Next he discusses the 1991 Gulf War but uses a video clip of the toppling of Saddam's statue in 2003 as support. Finally, he talks about how Ahmadinejad is quietly infiltrating the hierarchy of the Iranian government with "Twelvers," the Shiite sect to which he belongs.

Beyond his confusing the first Iraq War with the second, I am struck by two aspects of this segment. When he spoke of Saddam's WMD program he said, "We strongly suspected that Saddam had nuclear devises or was trying to acquire them." It strikes me that if America only "strongly sus-pected," we would have been less eager to go to war. Mr. Lindsey seems to adjust, in light of later revelations, the rationale for attacking Iran. One wonders what term he would have used if the broadcast was made just prior to or during the incursion.

In regard to the "Twelvers," Lindsey attempts to convince us that this is a small, radical sect of Islam. In actuality, over 80 percent of all Shiite Muslims are considered to be Twelvers. It would have been very difficult for Ahmadinejad to find someone for a government post who was *not* a Twelver.

In this part of the show, Lindsey claims that the health problems of Ariel Sharon and Ehud Olmert are punishments from God for handing over the Gaza Strip to the Palestinians. He suggests that the same fate might also await leaders of the United States who pressure Israel to make concessions to the Muslims. I find myself having a visceral reaction to this last statement. When Mr. Lindsey talks of the health problems of people beyond our borders, it is one thing. When he talks about our own leaders, it is quite another matter. I readily acknowledge the faulty logic here.

In his discussion Lindsey tells us that "every recent Israeli leader who has attempted to give back the land that God restored to Israel in 1967 has met with either personal physical catastrophe or personal political failure." It seems to me that the same can be said for those Israeli leaders who did *not* attempt to give back the land.

In the third segment, Mr. Lindsey attempts to convince us that the attack on 9/11, Hurricane Katrina, and the California wildfires of 2007 were all "correlated precisely with each time [the United States] has forced Israel to surrender land." He gives us only three options for these disasters: "Now whether these disasters are God's judgment, God's chastening, or God's warning to our country, I can't say. But to say that there is no correlation stretches the definition of coincidence."

Surely there are other options at hand. These coincidences could be just that. Further, I know of no situation where the United States "forced" Israel to surrender land.

Between segments, Lindsey makes a plea for financial support from his viewers. He claims that he is a "watchman on the wall" and that "Christ will soon return for his church and I want you to be ready to go." So he needs to get the *Hal Lindsey Report* into as many homes as possible. This can "be accomplished only with help from partners like you." His boldest claim is that "your participation makes it possible for me to report the Truth and warn the nations that the end of this age is near."

It seems to me that Lindsey uses his "prophesies" to create a sense of urgency in his viewers so that they will not hesitate to send money to support his ministry. How good a prophet has he been in the past? A second reading of *The Late, Great Planet Earth* will point out pretty quickly that he hasn't done a real bang-up job as prophet, and I'm sure he is grateful that God's punishment for false prophets seems to have been relaxed. It has been a very long time since a false prophet has been put to death because his prophesy did not become true. Don't get me wrong. I'm not suggesting that false prophesy be made a capital offense.

I suppose that the greatest benefit from this exercise has come from taking a closer look at my own faith: what I hold dear, what I proclaim, what I support financially. If someone were to examine my words with respect to the values I hold, they would probably find inaccuracies, un-substantiated claims, misquotations, etc., just as I have with Mr. Lindsey's words. It is much easier to hold the magnifying glass than it is to be the one inspected under it.

Finally, as I reflect on my words I realize, once again, that I am not real good at dispensing grace. Thanks be to God that He differs from me in that respect.

Back to Nadia.

Joel Osteen Ministries
(McPreachy's good-time prosperity piñata)
7:00 p.m.

My guest Michelle: I was raised in a pastor's home, part of a Christian fundamentalist denomination, where my frequent questions of doubt brought yet another offer of a Phillip Yancey or C. S. Lewis book. I graduated from Bible College and faithfully took my place in the ministry, beside my husband, and the doubts were kept just under the surface for decades. Whether brought on by my a desire for a more authentic and honest faith or the perils of raising four teenagers, my last few years of soul searching brought me to the edge of faith, to the abyss of atheism. My journey as an atheist was rather short-lived (three weeks to be precise), for I found the presence of doubt equally compelling as an atheist (how can one prove God doesn't exist?). I am currently reconstructing my faith, finding a way to accept the profound mystery that exists on either side of the faith coin. I find myself being ever more challenged by the extravagant love and grace of God that I have experienced in many ways, particularly through the person and mystery of Jesus Christ (in history and in Spirit). I consider myself a recovering fundamentalist, eager to embrace authentic and honest belief free of religious obligations or arrogance. I experience God most distinctly in moments of shared love, compassion, and grace. For now, that seems to be the most authentic and honest place of faith that I can place my trust.

◆◆◆

I'm happy to be getting back to the preaching, and preaching I am to get: Joel Osteen or, as I like to call him, McPreachy. My new friend Michelle has joined me. She has a deep heart that still stings from having just left a very conservative form of Christianity.

The opening is a standard soft-focus montage of painfully clean-cut folk with big happy smiles. These are the Osteenites, and they have drunk from McPreachy's Kool-Aid fountain of positive thinking. The commercial jingle prepares us for what's coming: "You're an overcomer, more than a conqueror, today...discover the champion in you." Is this basketball camp, or church? Joel's "church" sits in a sixteen-thousand-seat worship facility that was the former Compaq Center, then home of the Houston Rockets. It is estimated that over thirty-eight thousand people attend services each week at Lakewood Community Church. There are times when the popularity of someone like Joel Osteen is very confusing to me. But then I realize: there are times when the popularity of Hot Pockets is also confusing to me, so I choose not to dwell on it.

The camera pans over the multitude all clapping and cheering as the show is about to begin.

Joel comes out, and his particular level of clean-cutness makes Pat Boone look like Sid Vicious.

Joel stands on an enormous stage; behind him is a large spinning metal globe. I'm not sure what the purpose of the globe is, but it's undeniably reminiscent of the monumental flag behind George C. Scott in *Patton.*

"We love you. We know God has great things in store for you. We pray for you every single day." Joel starts where his colleagues end: the declaration of both their heartfelt love for you and of God's magic prosperity piñata in the sky filled with new cars, better jobs, big-screen TVs, and whiter teeth, just waiting for you to hit it with the right stick (stick and instructions included in Osteen's newest book).

He opens his sermon with...a blonde joke.

Osteen then holds up his Bible and his audience follows suit, repeating what he says (say it like you mean it, he exhorts):

This is my Bible. (*This is my Bible . . .*) I am what it says I am. I have what it says I have. I can do what it says I can do. Today I will be taught the word of God. I boldly confess my mind is alert; my heart is receptive. I will never be the same. In Jesus' name.

◆◆◆

Michelle: "It feels kind of unsafe to see that many people listening to just one person. All those people opening their mind to what just this one guy is saying."

Michelle apologizes in advance for the fact that she may become deeply sad about this, which, she admits, is the other side of anger. Unlike Michelle and other postevangelical friends of mine, I left conservative Christianity over twenty years ago, and am not carrying around the same feeling of betrayal. They often seem to look back in remorse at how they had participated in and even perpetuated an ideology that they now reject as false, or even abusive. That's a lot to carry. I so often hear people say, "I can't believe some of the things I used to say to young people when they came to me, the same things I now resent others for having said to me when I came to them."

Osteen: "Today I want to talk to you about living the abundant life."

I'm shocked.

An ad scrolls at the bottom of the screen for Osteen's latest book, *Become a Better You*, only $25.

Osteen says that people ask him if he is a prosperity minister, and he says no but that he's also not a poverty minister.

"God wants to take you to new levels, but you have to do your part and enlarge your thinking: I'm coming up higher; I'm going to step into that overflow anointing; I'm going to live the abundant life."

And this separates you from prosperity gospel preachers *how?*

◆◆◆

Osteen: "God pleasures in prospering you." The grammar of that sentence is so disturbing to me. But Michelle is disturbed on a whole other level. "I went to visit a friend recently," she starts to tell me, "who goes to one of these prosperity gospel churches. The preacher had people pull out their wallets to pray over them, and the more he got into talking about the wealth coming their way the more worked up they got, and they repeated his words just like this. Afterward I was just weeping; my friends thought I was moved by the spirit, but I just had this deep level of despair and

disdain and sadness — that *this* is what the message of Jesus has become."
Exactly.

◆◆◆

Talking about his father's impoverished childhood, Osteen describes
how his father made the decision that his children would not experience
such want. "In those days as a young minister, he was taught that you had
to be poor in order to be holy. In the churches he pastored, he did his
part and stayed holy and they did their part and kept him poor."

This is a difficult issue. On the one hand I can feel a bit resentful
toward churches who pay their pastors as little as possible even while they
themselves make much more money with much less education — not to
mention no seminary debt. But do I think pastors should be living lives
of conspicuous consumption? No. The thing that should keep me from
feeling too smug is that there is a continuum of conspicuous consumption,
and the life I lead, as well as the life Joel Osteen leads, are both on that
continuum.

All day I've heard these preachers pull out the same few verses to justify
their message of prosperity: the one (and I believe only) verse from any of
the gospels, John 10:10, "The thief comes only to steal and kill and destroy;
I came that they may have life, and have it abundantly." The problem
is that Osteen just said it this way: "Jesus came so that we may have
an abundant life." No. That we might have *life* and have it abundantly.
Whenever Jesus does actually talk about wealth, it is cautionary. "Do not
store up for yourselves treasures on earth." "Sell all you have and give it to
the poor." "It is easier for a camel to go through the eye of a needle than
for a rich man to enter the kingdom of heaven." "Blessed are the poor."
I know I'm prooftexting right back here, but in my Lutheran theological
tradition, the gospels trump other scripture, so using verses in the Old
Testament concerning God's blessing of Abraham or David to say that
Jesus wants us all to be rich and that the "blessing God promises" you is
financial prosperity is just weird.

I'm amazed at the almost total disregard for Christ's teachings on TBN.
In all the scripture references over the past fourteen hours, there has been
very little mention of Jesus. Sure, his name has been thrown around like
a talisman ("I claim the goodies in God's prosperity piñata in Jeeesus'
name"). But no one seems interested in the incarnation, life, teachings,
ministry, passion, cross, and resurrection of Jesus and what those things
tell us about who God is and who we are. I have heard no preaching from
the gospels today perhaps because there are no big-screen TVs or Bentleys

involved in the gospel of Jesus Christ. This all reminds me of a bumper sticker I saw recently: "Jesus called. He wants his name back."

◆◆◆

Osteen goes on. "Be a person of excellence, get to work on time, do 100 percent even when folks aren't watching, learn to work under God and not under people. When you sow these kinds of seeds, you're going to come into this overflow anointing."

This is his secret teaching about God's plan for your life? Common sense, no? I'm reminded of once years ago when I was coming down with a stomach bug. I was in the midst of finals and certain my stomach only hurt due to stress. I commenced with my day trying to put it out of my head. That only worked so long until I had to concede that I was actually sick. I became increasingly woozy on the drive home. I almost made it, but I passed out and ended up in the neighbor's driveway. When I came to, there was not enough blood in my brain to think, "Stop driving," so I put it in reverse, backed up over the mailboxes, and ended up in the other neighbor's flower bed, which was buried under a foot of snow. Apparently I got out of the car and passed out next door in a snow bank (according to the elderly couple across the street, who called an ambulance). When I came to the second time, paramedics were loading me into their rig. At the hospital the doctor ran a huge series of tests, which I was certain would reveal that I have some horrible exotic disease. Instead, when the doctor came back he said, "Ms. Bolz-Weber, you are actually a normal, healthy, boring, person. It's just that when you are sick, you should go home and lie down." (That little piece of expert advice cost me around $1,000.) The point being, you could spend the money to buy all of Osteen's books and CDs and conferences, *or* you could talk to any high school guidance counselor on earth who will tell you the same thing. Absolutely, you are more likely to do well if you dress the part, work hard, and show up on time. This, however, has nothing to do with God holding on to some kind of supernatural winning lotto ticket with your name on it.

◆◆◆

Describing the "overflow anointing" that he and his wife, Victoria, have received, being "blessed" beyond their dreams, Osteen says that this anointing is coming to you too if you just stay in faith. "You're coming in to new seasons of increase, new seasons of favor."

This guy talks like some sort of big smiley fortune cookie from God. ("You will be coming into overflow anointing — lucky numbers 2, 6, 17, 90, 97.")

Advertisement: A Night of Hope Tour, $15.

♦♦♦

A cute story follows of Osteen shopping with a friend. Every time the friend encountered something he wanted to buy he'd say, "Oh, but I can't afford it." Annoyed, Osteen said, "Would you stop saying that? At least say, 'I can't afford it . . . right now.' It's just a matter of time. I know because I'm faithful God will give me the desires of my heart, but if you have a poor mind, you'll have a poor life. [grasshoppa]"

Advertisement: Book: *Become a Better You*, $25.

♦♦♦

Deuteronomy 28:1–2, 11: "If you do as God wills, you will be blessed . . . , everything you do will prosper."

"All these blessings depend on the first verse: 'If you fully obey the Lord your God.' Obedience is the key to receiving God's blessings. Partial obedience is what keeps people in mediocrity."

What exactly is obedience to him? Obedience to what? If obedience means complying with all the rules in the Bible, and obviously we're talking Old and New Testament here, then perhaps he should talk to A. J. Jacobs, who documented his attempt to live according the rules of the Bible in his book *The Year of Living Biblically*. Jacobs, an agnostic Jew, read the entire Bible with a notepad next to him on which he wrote down every rule, guideline, and stricture in the biblical text. He then spent an entire year of his life trying to live "biblically." It's a brilliant book worth reading, but Jacobs's conclusion is that it is not possible. There are so many rules — a great number of which contradict each other or would have severe legal implication if actually adhered to — that everyone, no matter what they say, has to choose. So on what basis do you choose? I choose based on Christ. Who he was . . . who I am based on who he is . . . what he taught . . . what his life, death, and resurrection mean in terms of who I am and who God is. It is on this basis that I decide what holds water theologically and what does not. Love your enemies? Yes. Kill disobedient children? Not so much. These are both "rules" in the Bible.

Advertisement: Order this message on CD: $16.

Osteen proceeds to talk about the Jubilee year as described in Deuteronomy, an event that occurred every seven years during which the Hebrew people who were enslaved due to unpaid debt were freed despite what they owed. His biblical math is way off here. Jubilee happens every fifty years. This tells Osteen that God doesn't want us to be slaves to anything. "I sense in my spirit that we're entering into one of those seventh years. The seventh year begins new seasons of increase. God's going to break bondages that have held you back: debt, sickness, addiction, depression, mediocrity. You have to do your part and get this on the inside and believe."

◆◆◆

I've decided to get some more of the chips and salsa on the inside now, and I sense in my spirit that it will be yummy.

◆◆◆

"If you stay in faith," Osteen is telling us, "you're going to come into supernatural increase. When you walk in obedience, his blessings are going to chase you down and overcome you. I believe something supernatural happens when it is spoken over us so, I am going to speak it over you: a supernatural abundance of health, joy, and in your finances. You are being released into increase; the tide of the battle is turning. God is accelerating his blessings into your life; an abundance of good things is coming your way. I declare it in the name of Jesus, and if you receive it can you shout, Amen?"

Michelle: "This concept of how life should be makes us have a corporate narcissistic personality disorder."

Two points for Michelle.

THE ROUNDUP

Old Testament passages cited: Five.

New Testament passages cited: Four.

Cost of products offered: A bargain for "overflow anointing": $116.

Running total after 14½ hours: $7046.09

God: Wants you to be rich, but is waiting for you to believe it and start dressing professionally, showing up to work on time, giving 100 percent, and having a productive attitude. Then God will get more money for you. Oh, wait. That's actually you doing it. Don't tell Osteen.

Jesus: Came to earth so that you can be rich. Feel free to use his name to declare this.

Thought for this half-hour: If found in the memo line of an email, would the terms "supernatural increase" or "God pleasures in prospering you," or "enlarge your thinking, come up higher" make it past even the weakest of spam filters?

Ever Increasing Faith
(Every word in the Bible is true.
We know this because the Bible says it's true,
and, as we already said, every word of the Bible is true.)
7:30 p.m.

The *Ever Increasing Faith* show features the Prices, a family of African American preachers, with father, mother, and son on screen. The show opens with the theme: "With the power of faith, you can do the impossible." Images roll by of sad African Americans being transformed into happy ones while the word "Victory" scrolls across the screen. As the song moves to the words, "With the power of faith you can live a victorious life changing one life after another," the words on the screen are replaced with, "Transform your life." Perhaps another thirty-minute pep talk?

◆◆◆

We join Dr. Frederick Price (three guesses where that doctorate is from and whether or not it's honorary) in the middle of a sermon. He has a deeply kind, authentic voice. (If you guessed that its an honorary doctorate from Oral Roberts University, you win!)

"You have to constantly guard your thought life. It's a constant effort, a 24/7/365 job. Because your mind is open to the influence of the enemy, just like it is open to the influence of God."

Revelation 12:7–8: "Knowledge and its proper use wins battles."

Price seems more like a regular person and less like a showman than the previous preachers. He's an older African American man who is obviously preaching to his own congregation. There is no showboating here, just simple verse-by-verse preaching. When he calls out a scripture, he waits, says a few more things, then says, "If you got it say, 'I got it!'" They comply with "I got it!" Then he reads the verses from the Bible he carries while preaching. Sometimes liturgical types like myself can criticize the evangelical worship style as too passive for everyone but the pastor. They don't say things back and forth like in the liturgy, or come forward and kneel for communion, or cross themselves, or pass the peace. But here there is a liturgical feel based in the biblicism of the community; it's actually kind of lovely.

He's preaching about how the devil tries to deceive us.

Michelle: "I didn't realize that it wasn't until after the book of Daniel was written that there was a belief about life after death, heaven and hell."

True, which makes maintaining the belief that every part of the Bible holds equal authority a bit problematic, as one would simultaneously have to believe in an afterlife and not even consider it as a possibility.

It's hour fifteen and I'm feeling a little hazy. I know there are things he's saying that ten hours ago would have drawn some snarky comment from me, but at this point I let them all go, like pitches straight over the plate, one after the other.

◆◆◆

"How do you relate to the Bible at this point in your life?" I ask Michelle.

"I absolutely love it," Michelle responds. "It speaks to me all the time. Even in my doubts I would go to the Bible, and it would speak to me. I know now that this is because it holds a profound truth that has nothing to do with facts. Now I don't face a dilemma when I read it, as I did when I felt like I had to believe it literally."

"That's really beautiful, but is it difficult sometimes for you given where you came from theologically?"

Michelle: "Knowing God and his truth has become more important to me than a factual knowledge of my Bible, and that's a scary place to come to. But it felt like a paradigm shift. Like I was standing on the rings of Saturn and was flipped over thinking I was going to fall, but lo and behold I was still standing."

The change to a broader view of faith has been both liberating and difficult for Michelle. As she tells it: "This has been challenging for my kids, who were raised with heaven and hell. One of them said something about someone going to hell, and I said that some people think differently about hell. What if God has the future covered and what God really wants is for us to be transformed by love and to love God and others. This was really hard for them to hear, especially from their mom, who upheld the hell teaching for so long."

I can't imagine the ambiguity she is living in, but I'm really glad she's here.

◆◆◆

Michelle: "Sometimes I still wonder if I'm falling into the deception of the end times, but then I know deep down that I'm safe. These scriptures have filled my mind with fear and guilt about veering into danger."

It is insidious — the view of scripture Michelle is talking about. God wrote the Bible; everything therein is factual, even the parts that seem wrong, immoral, confusing, or contradictory. If even for a moment you doubt this, it is because Satan is trying to trick you. How do we know this? Because the Bible said it, and God wrote the Bible.

♦♦♦

Price: "Are you guarding your thought life? When he comes, you're going to think you thought the thought up, but if you have your armor and Bible knowledge properly used, you will quit when you ought to."

♦♦♦

Michelle: "This battle of the mind stuff is just what I would try to make my doubts about. It was just spiritual warfare, and I had to overcome. I had to hold up a standard against Satan. I would battle constantly. When you're in that though, in the 'in group' and you kind of surrender to the superficiality of it, it feels safer in the black and white. But when life happens like it does, and so much of your life ends up in the gray zone instead of the black and white, there is this constant dissonance inside you. You eventually just have to shut off the desire for authenticity."

Me: "I was raised with that too. Like if you don't believe this then you're going to hell. But you can't *make* yourself believe it."

Michelle: "You can try, like me for decades."

Advertisement: For your love gift of $15 or more for DVD and $20 or more for VHS you can receive a recording of Dr. Price's message from today.

Book on Ephesians from Dr. Price: *Harness the Supernatural Power You Need to Live a Victorious Life:* $10.95.

CD: *Overcoming Temptations, Trials, and Tests.* "God guarantees us victory in every trial or test, but you have to know how to apply God's word in order to realize that victory in your life." Three-CD set: $14.95 or more.

THE ROUNDUP

Old Testament passages cited: Zero, but talked about Adam and Eve a lot.

New Testament passages cited: Fourteen.

Cost of products offered: $60.90.

Running total after 15 hours: $7106.99

God: It doesn't really matter about God. It's all up to us.

Jesus: No mention.

Thought for this half-hour: What is the difference between actually believing something and making ourselves believe something because we feel we have to?

Praise the Lord
(*Heartbreaking, inspiring,*
limbless day on PTL)
8:00 p.m.

My guest Kristen Lothman: I am a meandering twenty-something currently living in Denver. I grew up in the Presbyterian Church (PCUSA). My father is an ordained Presbyterian minister but does not have a church; he runs a small interfaith counseling center in Florida. And so I grew up with one foot in the church, one foot out. I am in the process of returning to school to pursue a master's in social work with a clinical practice concentration. My dream job is to counsel individuals who have been wounded or condemned by abusive religiosity.

◆◆◆

The *PTL* intro portrays a large gold globe of the earth with pictures of Paul and Jan Crouch in Europe, Asia, Africa — you get the picture. I'm finding myself almost giddy with expectation of seeing the lady with the large pink hair, the emblem of American televangelism, she and Tammy Faye, the mascara-streaked showgirls of religious broadcasting. But my excitement fades as the opening for this *PTL* episode makes it clear that there will be no Jan Crouch; it is, instead, limbless day on TBN. Looks like we are in for a man without legs, a man without arms, a man with half an arm, a paraplegic, a blind woman, a man without arms or legs, and finally a white able-bodied gospel singer who looks as if she is in a fairly deep depression.

The show's host, Paul Crouch Jr., makes the misplaced claim right off the bat that we are all disabled in some way, adding cutely that for him, "It's mostly mental." I think this was meant to be light, self-deprecating humor, but his "we're all disabled" seems misplaced in the context of a studio full of people in wheelchairs.

The *PTL* set is a knock-off of every other evening talk show, just without a great band and funny host. Instead we've got a couple of middle-aged white evangelicals and lots of folks in wheelchairs. Behind the sofa (which is an amazing blue modern piece, which I honestly think is fabulous) is the obligatory blinking skyline, but none of us can figure out which city it's representing. Kristen is asking what my guess would be. "I don't know," offering my best guess, "the New Jerusalem?"

116

They cut to Tony Melendez, an armless man playing the guitar with his feet. The song — I could not make this up — is "They Are Holding Hands in Heaven," which seems a bit unfair to the armless. But what do I know? I'm feeling voyeuristic at this point because with an armless guy playing the guitar in front of me, I couldn't stop watching if I tried to.

The first guest is familiar to me, which I'm not expecting. It takes about thirty seconds before I realize where I know her from. Oh, my gosh, it's "Joni." Joni Erikson was paralyzed as a result of a diving accident at age seventeen. She is famous in the evangelical world and ours was far from the only family whose bookshelf included the book *Joni,* a little paperback from the 1970s with the title written in her own "mouth writing." She became an artist who grasped whatever writing or painting implement she needed with her mouth. She's beautiful and articulate and full of sincerity, saying things like, "To embrace life is to embrace Christ" and "God shows up best in our weakness." She was a hero to me when I was growing up, a real inspiration. Little did I know that one day I'd be in a position of critically analyzing her, which of course I could never make myself do. I wasn't expecting to see someone from my Church of Christ upbringing, and even I can't be cynical about this woman.

Joni's talking about what her faith was like at seventeen before the accident and how she just kind of "kept Jesus in her back pocket" and that she had thought she was "doing God a huge favor" by accepting him. But when she was depressed to the point of suicide in the hospital following the news that she would never again be able to use her hands or legs, faith was a different matter. She eventually prayed a simple prayer to God to help show her how to live. "I didn't get many answers," she recalls. "But God knew I didn't need a whole lot of words, but I needed the *Word,* Jesus Christ, the man of sorrows, acquainted with grief. He felt the sting when I was hurting."

Joni is a theologian of the cross indeed. She sees that God uses this wheelchair as a chisel to whittle away her self-reliance; she still wakes up thinking that she just doesn't have what it takes to do this paraplegic thing, but that then she remembers that God does have what it takes. "I am just someone who is ready to acknowledge how much I need God and need him desperately."

To which PC Jr. says, "It's amazing in all the things you do around the world, helping others and donating wheelchairs to those in need, how much God can do *despite* the wheelchair." Is he even listening to her? It seems to me that what she is saying is that God uses her *because* of the wheelchair.

Joni tells how she never refuses prayer, and apparently a whole lot of well-meaning and enthusiastic "prayer warriors" offer to pray for her healing. She doesn't refuse, but she insists that what she would really like to be prayed for is that she be healed from the times when "I cherish inflated ideas of my own importance... the times when I fudge the truth... the times when I manipulate my husband to get things my own way... sin. Ma'am if you want to pray for me, pray that I receive the power of the resurrection to put to death the things in my life that displease him. The desire of my heart is to get rid of sin so that my state in heaven is all the more full. That's the healing I'm after." Joni Erikson should have her own show. I'm kind of dumbfounded by her humility, and it's about all I've seen of this particular character trait in the last fifteen hours, including from myself. Michelle seems struck as well and says, "It's obvious that this very fundamental faith has really brought her enrichment." I feel a little conflicted because she said so many beautiful, humble, true things that convicted me, and yet ended it by saying she wanted to get rid of her sin so that she can have a better place in heaven. I'm not sure we can actually get rid of sin, and even if we could I don't think the hereafter includes merit-based upgrades. Still, Joni is a gentle, genuine soul.

Joni turns to the camera and tells us, the audience, "You can smile, not despite your disabilities but because of them." Tinkling piano starts again. "God is in the middle of your suffering and may not give you the reasons for your suffering, but will give you Jesus, the Word, the man of sorrows who bore your sin so that you may bear your cross. And that sweet mystical union with him at that point is ecstasy beyond words. It is worth anything, even quadriplegia, to be his friend." I'm hoping at this point that PC Jr. has heard her. She's saying that God's work in the world can be done even through suffering, that we get to participate in God's work *because* of our brokenness, not despite our brokenness. I tend to agree with her. I know for myself that the uglier things about me — my inordinate love of booze (before getting sober fifteen years ago), my sarcasm, the fact that I swear like a truck driver, and even the fact that I have tattoos all the way down my arm — these inelegant aspects of myself that would never pass TBN muster, that seem "non-Christian," are exactly the things that others in my community find compelling. These character traits are seen by nicey-nice Christianity as "worldly," but God still finds them useful. Joni seems different from all else I've seen today in that she admits that she still struggles, but any of their own sinfulness hinted at or explicitly named by most of these TBN folks seems always located in the past.

The next guest, James Bertrand, lost his arm to a suicide attempt when he injected horse tranquilizer into it. I'm a sucker for that kind of story, so I'm already on his side a little bit. He claims that when he tried to kill himself he was out of his mind, but now for him to have "committed to 'serving the Lord,'" he must be out of his mind still. Amen! Whooo! Praise the Lord! Can it be anything other than pandering if one continually shouts "Praise the Lord" on the *Praise the Lord Show?* "We're just going to serve God like we're out of our minds." Mission accomplished.

"Can somebody give God a handclap of praise . . . whoooo!" Note to self: when I'm preaching and I feel like the congregation is not responding to me by saying Amen or laughing at my jokes, when I'm just not feelin' the love so to speak, I'll just tell 'em to "give the Lord some applause." Then if they don't it'll mean they don't love Jesus. This is going to be really helpful to me on Sundays when I'm crashing and burning in the pulpit.

PC Jr.: "Once again, that Satan wanted you dead big time, didn't he? And the reason is why?" I'm superexcited that I'm about to hear the inner thoughts of Satan. It's strange for me how much these people talk about what God thinks and wants and what Satan thinks and wants. It's as though they are collectively the omniscient narrator of the cosmos. They tell us what the main characters, God and Satan, are thinking so that the narrative will make sense to us. So here is why Satan wanted James Bertrand dead. (The plot thickens. . . .) "The *Just for Jesus* crusade, Paul." Bertrand has found a legal way of taking children out of their public school on a field trip to "come worship God." "If they are discriminated against," Bertrand says, "they can sue the school system. Give God a handclap of praise for that."

PC Jr.: "You are not an attorney. How did God give you this revelation?"

"Well one day I woke up with an impression that God wanted to use the kids to reach the city."

It turns out that all field trips are voluntary and parents have to sign off on each one. If you can take a field trip with the Key Club, kids in Bible clubs can do field trips too. "If we can get an excused absence to go to a dental appointment," says Bertrand, "and if we can get an excused absence to go to a Planned Parenthood appointment, then we can get an excused absence to worship God."

◆◆◆

Dear Principal Riley,

Please excuse Paul Jr. from school today. He is worshiping God. After that he'll be at a Planned Parenthood appointment and then the dentist.

Mrs. Crouch

◆◆◆

They show a clip of an event in Baton Rouge with thousands of kids flooding onto the stage. Bertrand "felt" like someone there was thinking about suicide that day. Okay, so seventy-five hundred public school kids from Baton Rogue — the fact that a few might want out of their lives is not a revelation from God; it's eighth-grade social studies. He thought that he was going to "just give an invitation to salvation." An invitation? Like the work of Christ is his own personal gated community and he's going to call and invite these kids over. "Hey, come over for some salvation. There'll also be plenty of hot dogs on the grill and a heated pool. Just buzz me when you get here." Instead he asked these seventy-five hundred kids from Baton Rogue if there was somebody thinking of suicide, and seventy-five kids stood up. Maybe this guy really cares about these kids and thinks he is doing the best thing he can for them by giving them an hour of Jesus during their school day, and he may be right. But I just wonder what it matters in the end? Do they "get saved" and then just go back to whatever impoverished life they came from? Maybe a pep rally for the Lord gives them a hope that they aren't getting anywhere else. I know I'm not doing anything for these kids, so I should probably shut up now.

◆◆◆

The armless guitar-playing guy (who has a business called Toe Jam Music) sings another song while playing guitar with his feet. The song includes the lyrics "Open your arms and fall into his grace...." Ironic. But then again, his song also includes a lyric about how Jesus turns water into wine, "good wine," which is a theology I'm totally down with. Basically if you are the incarnated Almighty God, why turn water into boxed Pink Zinfandel?

◆◆◆

Jennifer Rothschild is a very attractive woman in I would guess her early forties. She's articulate and well dressed in the standard suit and short hair. She doesn't have the mannerisms of many blind people, which we learn is because she was sighted until her midteens. At the age of fifteen Rothschild was diagnosed with a degenerative eye disease, which eventually took her sight. She describes the moment she was diagnosed, when the doctor said "blindness." "This is a word like 'cancer' or 'divorce' that you never want to be associated with," and when she heard the word it "fell to the bottom of my soul and scraped everything on the way down that used to be secure. It is a real struggle. I mean blindness stinks, to put it real unspiritually."

Why is saying that something as devastating as blindness stinks "putting it unspiritually"? Is the "spiritual" associated only with the positive? Is that a sustainable worldview?

PC Jr.: "Did you ever cry at night and blame God and think 'Why me?'" To which she says no, because of the way in which God "planted his word" in her soul. She has never been angry with God because she knows intuitively that she needs God so much. She talks about how we have a choice, and when suffering and hardship come into our lives we can either choose to build up a wall between us and our only source of strength or we can use those same bricks to build a bridge to God. I think she is right on some level, though question the fact that it is apparently not spiritual to be angry with God. Why this idea that the spiritual is happy and pleasant and nice and the unspiritual is angry and frustrated and difficult? What about the place of lament in our tradition? We can actually be angry with God and stand on the firm foundation of the tradition of others who have cried, "How long, O God, will you hide your face from me?" This is not unspiritual, and, frankly, God can take it. But then I think I might be starting to get it. All of these folks keep talking about the fact that their disability makes them understand how much they need God, but the truth is that they do not need God any more or less than anyone else. It's just that their condition makes it more difficult for them to pretend otherwise.

PC Jr.: "You have been such an inspiration to me. This is unbelievable to know [piano tinkling] that no matter your circumstance, God will use you mightily. So [turning to the camera] put away your pity parties." I'm sorry, did an able-bodied white man who has inherited a multi-billion-dollar televangelism global empire just tell his viewers, the unemployed, the disabled, and the poor not to feel sorry for themselves? Wow. Well, I guess he should know, right?

Kristen has been watching silently but now wonders aloud. "What do you have to concede theologically to be on this show? The host just said that this woman has faith and is positive so stop throwing a pity party. I don't think it's helpful for people that they aren't allowed to have their grief." I think she may have a point. I know at least for myself if I was depressed about my life, seeing people who were missing limbs but had plenty of faith wouldn't snap me out of it so much as make me depressed now for a whole new reason — because now I'm a schmuck too.

So if you are TBN and you've had on an armless guy, a quadriplegic, a blind woman, and a legless guy, what would be your next move? That's right. A man with no arms or legs. PC Jr. is now conversing with a man who has no limbs. His name is Nick Vujicic, a very handsome, intelligent young Australian who was born without arms and legs for no apparent medical reason. He's articulate and funny and entirely likeable.

PC Jr.: "Did you have times when you were like, 'Why me?'"

Nick: "There were some Sundays I didn't want to hear the preacher — 'We were all created in God's image.' I didn't see that. I had faith, much more than a mustard seed, and all I wanted was arms and legs. I wanted to have joy, and the only reason I didn't have joy in my life was because I had no arms or legs. I thought if only, if only.... But I found out that even if God changes our circumstances, guess what: there's another circumstance coming and the real victory is when you are a conqueror and set free from the bondage of the circumstance. We go from glory to glory in the spiritual." Okay, now I am actually inspired. This kid is truly amazing. He seems very sincere. He doesn't seem to be conceding a theological viewpoint at all.

PC Jr.: "What were your dreams as a kid?"

Nick: "Man, I'm so jealous of what's his name with the guitar!"

PC Jr.: "Tony Melendez?"

Nick: "Yeah, I want some guitar lessons with this thing. [He lifts up the little foot-type thing on his stump; it's a narrow heel with a toe or two.] If anyone can teach me it would be that guy. Hopefully, he won't charge me an arm and a leg because I have none." Now I know I love him. "Actually I don't even have big dreams. I would just love to run or to go as far as I can on a bike. I'd like to know how it feels to smash into a pole with a bike. I had a lot of anger and depression and bitterness toward God, like when people would come up to me and say, 'You know Nick, everything is going to be okay.' But you *don't* know how it feels. This is what I'm dying to hear, what everyone is dying to hear, that you are loved and everything is going to be okay."

PC Jr.: "God is using you mightily *despite* your circumstances." And now I really just want to shoot this guy who obviously is not even listening to these amazing people he is interviewing. No one has implied that they are doing God's work in the world *despite* their circumstance — not one.

I wonder if the guests are having similar reactions. I then realize that Kristen is thinking the same thing. She asks, "Is it me or is he not getting it?" Now I know I don't have Stockholm Syndrome because if I did I would be feeling sympathy with my captors, and what I really am feeling toward PC Jr. is contempt, which as we now know is very "unspiritual."

PC Jr. asks *the question:* "Would you get arms and legs now if you could?"

Nick: "No. Knowing what I know now, I can honestly say no. So many people have been transformed by God's spirit through this empty vessel. It's not about Nick and about what you can or cannot do. It's about what God can do *through* you if you let him in."

This is beautiful theology. I love him. Okay, maybe more coffee would be good right now.

♦♦♦

Back to Tony Melendez, and I'm bracing for a song like, "Hold My Hand, Precious Lord." But in the very next thought I realize that hymn writer Fanny Crosby, who I'm convinced has to be one of God's favorites, was completely blind and wrote heartbreaking hymns including lines like, "Visions of rapture now burst on my sight" ("Blessed Assurance"). I suppose these tales of inspiration from those with strong faith and weak body are not so unusual. Crosby once said: "It seemed intended by the blessed providence of God that I should be blind all my life, and I thank him for the dispensation. If perfect earthly sight were offered me tomorrow I would not accept it. I might not have sung hymns to the praise of God if I had been distracted by the beautiful and interesting things about me."

♦♦♦

We go now from the musician with legs but no arms to Bob Weiland, a guy with arms and no legs. This is the second time we've seen Bob today. He is a Vietnam vet who lost his legs to a land mine.

PC Jr.: "I know that God has used you mightily despite your handicap. How would your life be different if you had not stepped one step to the right and missed that mortar shell?"

Now I know he's not listening since mortar shells are rarely booby-trapped. Mortar shells are shot at you. You don't step on something that is being fired at you. This guy is an idiot.

PC Jr.: "Was there ever a dark moment when you questioned God?"

Bob: "War is not a pretty picture. When I was in Vietnam everybody was trying to blow my head off, so I'm just glad that the Lord's grace brought me home."

He reads a letter he sent home from Vietnam:

Dear Mom and Dad,

I'm in the hospital. Everything is going to be okay. The people here are taking good care of me. It won't be that much of an adjustment. Please don't worry about me. Maybe I can help you out in real estate.

Love, Bob

P.S.: I think I lost my legs.

"I was weaving in and out of consciousness, but the sweet holy spirit was guiding me."

PC Jr.: "Bob you inspire me every time, my half-brother in the Lord."

◆◆◆

On to Arthur Blessitt: a preacher who has carried an actual cross all over the world, which makes me think he may be a bit confused.

Arthur is most famous for being involved with George W. Bush's conversion to Jesus in the 1980s. He is also rumored to be planning to cut a two-inch cross out of the twelve-foot cross he has carried all over the world and launch it's mini-me into space.

This guy takes "Jesus complex" to a whole new level. He tells a story of how he was carrying the cross on a New Zealand beach when a woman came up to him and said that she was going to run into the ocean but she asked God to give her a sign and she saw him carrying the cross and she felt new life. (Tinkling piano.)

PC Jr.: "If anything here touched you, there has been a number on the screen. Call that number and there will be a precious 'prayer partner' to pray with you. We need your love gifts large or small to keep TBN going."

Now I'm wondering if God uses Paul Crouch Jr. *despite* the fact that he can be an idiot, or *because* of the fact that he can be idiot. I'll just add that to my list of questions to ask Jesus in heaven.

Announcer: "Now, until next time, remember to praise the Lord."

Advertisement: "For your gift of $25 a month or a one-time gift of $250, Paul and Jan would like to give you this beautiful Holy Family Fabergé-style egg decorated with sparkling jewel-like emblems. This Fabergé-style egg is a special work of art. Open the doors, and inside is the Holy Family gathered around the Christ child." I'll take six.

That kind of sums up TBN at this point.

Thought for this hour: Does God use PC Jr. *because* he's an idiot, or *despite* the fact that he's an idiot?

Intermission

REFLECTION ON
THE BLANK SCREEN

What Is Really Being Sold on TBN?

FOR YOUR LOVE GIFT...someone will get healed, we'll save souls, servicemen and women will get the gospel in Iraq, the Christian Sudanese will be fed, we'll convert Muslims and reform criminals, and God will make you rich. These lofty promises are ever present on TBN and are arguably what people are really buying when they "plant their seed"; it is purpose itself, and not a Fabergé-style egg, that is being purchased. It's difficult not to picture the isolated elderly writing checks as one of their remaining acts of personal agency. These checks represent their ability to once again effect change, be a force, make a difference — actions not easily undertaken from one's living room under most circumstances. But TBN offers to do great things as your proxy in the world, spread the Word of God, feed the hungry, save the heathens, and guarantee a victorious, abundant, prosperous return on your investment. The meaning-making function of consumerism is present but inverted; rather than advertising that presents a product that promises meaning and fulfillment, the TBN audience is being pitched the meaning and fulfillment point blank; the product (books, Fabergé-style eggs, DVDs) is just thrown in.

(I do not realize until the last sentence of this particular insight that I have written every word while drinking from my National Public Radio coffee mug. Do I give money to NPR because I feel that I get to be a part of informing the whole nation? Does my NPR coffee mug represent a false sense of community? One might hear extensive use of the term "NPR community" during the insufferable pledge drives on public radio, and now I wonder to what degree this differs from Jesse Duplantis asking me to become one of his ministry partners.)

Against All Odds
(The session in which I pass out)
10:00 p.m.

I'm alone. No one is scheduled for the next show, *Against All Odds*, a dramatic reenactment of the establishment of the state of Israel. As I said earlier, this is a topic in which I have very little interest. I get that this makes me a bit of a moron, but I'm okay with that. I lie on the sofa trying not to...feel guilty about...having muted thhhhee...TV...and...now ...I'm ...zzzzzzzzzz

Life Focus
(*Exploring menopause with my ex-boyfriend*)
10:30 p.m.

My guest Eric Byrd lives in Colorado with his two sons. He's glad that somebody has finally inquired about the financial hoo-hah surrounding several of the country's megachurches and, if he were Republican or lived in Iowa, he would vote for Senator Grassley's reelection.

◆◆◆

...there's a knock at the door and I'm up with a start.

The knocker, Eric Byrd, is my ex-boyfriend and not the least bit Christian. We've just recently been in contact after about thirteen years. He's a single dad and tech writer. I'm surprised he agreed to be a part of my little project, but here he is at my house at 10:30 on a Friday night to watch Christian TV for an hour.

It doesn't take long after we've settled in to watch *Life Focus* to realize that the show we've chosen to watch is about menopause. It is difficult to overstate how uncomfortable this is.

◆◆◆

"Why is there a show about menopause on TBN?" Eric asks.

Oh, how I wish I had a different personality right now because then I could just be silently uncomfortable, but instead I say everything I'm thinking. At this late hour my editing mechanism is a bit shot. Like any other gal, I'd love for my ex-boyfriend to hold the illusion that somehow I have not aged since we were together. However, I don't want this to be true quite enough to actually have done any of the things women do when they want to look like they don't age. I don't dye my hair or have unspeakable things done to me surgically. Of course, having him come by closer to the beginning of this ordeal rather than the end might have helped the haggard-factor.

Naturally, I verbalize: "The older I get the more I realize this culture does not want women to age. There are countless products on the market designed to mask the fact that I have lived each day from the day of my birth consecutively. I'm keeping my gray hair and wrinkles. Screw it."

Eric: "Would you do the eyes?"

Oh my God, is he implying I need an eyelift?

"You know, the zzzzzz laser thing," he adds, motioning around his pupils.

Then I realize he's referring to my glasses and the potential of Lasik.

"Oh, yeah, I'm not a candidate for that."

◆◆◆

They're interviewing Ronna Snyder, a woman with trendy eyeglasses, blond blond hair, and huge earrings. She's a seriously hot older gal. In the midst of her menopause crisis of hot flashes and mood swings, she decided to confide in a woman (her "meno-mentor") who is slightly older than herself. "I won't tell you how old," Anderson smiles, "because us midlife women, we don't talk about those types of things." Midlife? There's no telling how old Ronna is, but she did mention that her symptoms started at age fifty-five so we know she's probably nearing sixty given that she's written and published a book, *Hot Flashes from Heaven,* about her menopause experience. So if that's midlife then she'll be a hot 120-year-old when she goes. Is the term "midlife" used to indicate the actual middle of one's potential age span, or should I not be taking that term so literally? Let's see. I'm thirty-eight. If I double that it's seventy-four, no, seventy-six. I think I'm delirious. And now I think I'm middle-aged.

Eric: "I know I'm not nearly the expert you are, but this isn't actually a Christian show, is it? Shouldn't there be more, I don't know, Jesus?"

"Actually there's precious little Jesus to be had on TBN apart from 'calling on his name' in order to get what you want out of him. Kind of like voodoo."

◆◆◆

Narrator: "This laughter and friendship between Ronna and her mentor was the key that helped charge Ronna to try something most menopausal women would never do." (Images of her snapping up a leather vest, wearing high-heeled boots, and straddling a motorcycle.)

Eric: " . . . becoming a stripper?"

The next shot: Ronna riding a Harley.

Ronna: "I am a hormonally challenged midlife broad who has somehow been able to get a grasp on victory over menopause. At least that's what I think today. Don't call me on a bad day."

I think she's fabulous.

She also cleaned out her closet of all the clothes that made her feel old or fat. She somehow pulls off the "I'm sixty and hot" look without that specific form of pathetic that comes from older women trying to look younger. She is no elderly teeny-bopper.

Matthew emerges from the basement where he's been writing a sermon. "How's menopause?" he asks.

Eric: "It's rough, man."

Me: "Yeah, but she bought a Harley, and I've just decided that's going to be our strategy too, honey." Matthew agrees.

◆◆◆

Narrator: "Caroline Brown (author of *The Black Woman's Guide to Menopause*) also found out that menopause is not necessarily the end but the beginning..."

Eric: "...of the end."

Narrator "...of new confidence and new strength."

Faced with the difficulties of menopause, Caroline went to her doctor.

Narrator: "What Caroline needed was estrogen replacement therapy."

Me: "...and good health insurance when she gets breast cancer."

Eric: "Yeah, I don't know about the estrogen thing."

Me: "Yeah, I say that now, but when it's happening to me, I'll probably be like 'give me the damn pills already.'"

◆◆◆

Thanks be to God, it's over now. Maybe if I'm superlucky the next hour will be all about menstruation or erectile dysfunction. That'd be great.

THE ROUNDUP

Old Testament passages cited: Zero.

New Testament passages cited: Zero.

Cost of products offered: DVD of show: $20.

Running total after 18 hours: $7126.99

God: Zero.

Jesus: Zero.

Watching a show with my ex-boyfriend about what happens to women's bodies when they age: Priceless.

Thought from the show: Start saving for that menopausal Harley.

After the credits, we are served up a clip from *Praise the Lord* in which a man in a mullet, mustache, and pink cardigan with large brown polka dots sings "Blessed Assurance" on the ornate *PTL* set.

Eric: "I like his sweater. Or is that his bathrobe?"

The camera fades in on a bad stained-glass wall. It looks like maybe Jan and Paul's grandkids made it in the oven, like one of those craft kits where kids pour the colored crystals into the metal forms and then bake it. I think it's Jesus, but he has white hair and a white robe.

Eric: "Is that Jesus, or Grizzly Adams?

I sing along: "Perfect submission . . . all is at rest."

Eric has a pleading look on his face, so I stop.

I ask Eric what he thinks of all this.

He answers, but without turning to me. (He is transfixed by the Polka Dot Man.) "Honestly I'm wondering when they'll wheel the casket in. This looks just like a funeral home. It doesn't seem like a church, and it doesn't feel like someone's actual living room, so it kind of looks like there's possibly an embalming studio downstairs."

"The number is on the bottom of the screen," I offer. "Do you want to call in?"

Eric: "No, I'd just start yelling."

"You could ask them to pray for that rage that's just about to spill out from the inside of your bad place."

The call-in idea is interrupted when I get a text message. It's from Rebecca Boardman, one of my remote viewing friends: "I want that sweater."

I am laughing about my wonderful friends out there today all pulling for me. Maybe six more hours won't be so bad.

The Dream Center with Tommy Barnett
*(Don't fake your own kidnapping
just because you're having an affair)*
11:00 p.m.

On the stage of what looks like a theater stands a young man — spiky hair, jeans, and hip blazer — who starts his sermon with the Webster's definition of "worry" and a lame joke about marriage. Definitions and jokes are the first two things we learned in seminary not to do. This is Matthew Barnett, pastor at the Dream Center at the Angelus Temple in Los Angeles.

The Angelus Temple. It takes me a minute to realize what that means. Then it comes. The Angelus Temple was built by Pentecostal pioneer Aimee Semple McPherson in the 1920s. Aimee is a fascinating character is U.S. religious history. She was tremendously popular in the tent revival preaching world, which needless to say was dominated by men. As with the origins of Pentecostalism, her ministry defied the barriers of race, color, gender, and ethnicity. Her Angelus Temple sat fifty-three hundred people filed up several times a week for revival services. Social welfare was of deep concern to McPherson, causing her to establish outreach ministries to aid those in the inner city who were in great need. That's the good. The bad is just as bad. In a now famous scandal, McPherson disappeared from a beach in California and went missing. Two people died looking for her body. Assuming she was dead, the media and her following went a little nuts, only for McPherson to reappear thirty-four days later in Mexico with stories of being abducted, tortured, and drugged. She claimed to have walked thirteen hours across a desert to freedom, despite the fact that her shoes bore no such marks and she was wearing a watch her mother had given her that she had not worn to the beach the day of her alleged abduction. In all fairness perhaps her abductors were of the considerate sort and allowed her to go home and pack first. It's hard to say. Her story of abduction was not at all helped by the fact that the manager of McPherson's Christian radio station, with whom she had a rather close friendship, also disappeared and reappeared at the same time. McPherson died in 1944 of a barbiturate overdose.

I also can't help but think about Ted Haggart, Jim Bakker, and the six televangelists under Senate investigation as I write; what is to be learned from those who fall from such moral heights? Shakespeare, if he were alive today, would populate his plays with such as these. I contend that there is a relationship between espousing personal holiness on such a large scale and the inability to appear less than what you claim. Do those who follow these charismatic leaders on some level *need* them to appear to be without sin? If so, is this need located in the projection of an ideal that then entices those who know they are so much less than that ideal, or is it so that when the inevitable happens, those who follow them can think, "Well, I'm not *that* sinful, so I must be okay"? More than anything I'm wondering if they started their careers as religious leaders as idealistic and earnest as myself, believing themselves servants of the gospel. Did they look at corruption in the church and think they would be different? If so, then what were the steps they took that landed them flat on their backs, fallen and shamed?

What were the little compromises, the little deceptions, the little betrayals of self and God that led to the big one that everyone noticed?

◆◆◆

The next thing I hear is the young preacher saying, "Our God is still Jehovah Jireh," which always has sounded a little dirty to me, not unlike so much of what I've heard on TBN today, e.g., "give your love gift," "sow your faith seed," etc.

"You may be in a tough place now," Pastor Barnett continues, "but you have a rich and powerful daddy." That's a bit too much like God as a member of the Village People for me to get on board. . . . God as a really hot construction worker who pleasures in prospering you . . . God as. . . . Yeah, I'm delirious.

I can't keep up with his rat-a-tat-tat delivery. He's gone from David to Jesus to Tyra Banks to R.E.M. to Psalms to Peter to marriage and back to David in the space of one minute, which I think is the reason he doesn't have time to say what scriptures he's quoting. Eric asks, "Can you tell which is from the Bible and what is just from him? It's a mixture right?" Yeah, it's definitely a mixture. His message that worry is not productive or useful is fine; it's just not really a sermon per se. He is really trying to be funny: "God even knows the number of hairs on you head and for some of you that's not so hard." To which Eric responds, "This must have been written after the writers' strike . . . um, is that a laugh track?"

"Worry is a sin," Barnett goes on to say, "and is not in the DNA of the children of God."

"I think it's actually a hard-wired part of being human," says Eric. "What if I do everything this guy says and I still have worry in my life? *Then* what's wrong with me?"

"Um, chemical imbalance?" I offer. Not helpful, so I go another route. "There is something Jesus said in the Bible, that no one by worrying can add a single hour to their life. I think that's true. Not thoughtfully considering the landscape of your life, *but real worry*, does it help us?"

Eric: "Maybe. Like by keeping us out of the path of traffic or from going to gun shows carrying anti-NRA placards. I don't worry. I just go straight to rage, and let me tell you, rage *will* add years to your life." I laugh. Eric and I met in AA in 1993, and despite the crazy relationship and breakup we are still fond of each other, especially the dark humor in our lives that comes with the recovering addict/alcoholic's life. He talks about being rageful and angry, but I know that's all inside; on the outside he's quite gentle.

Matthew Barnett winds up the sermon by misquoting the serenity prayer and then falsely attributing it to St. Francis, which Eric and I find terribly amusing, because unless St. Francis was really a guy named Reinhold Niebuhr who lived in the twentieth century, this is way off.

I decide to Google this Dream Center ministry and I'm kind of blown away at what I find. According to their website the Dream Center feeds over twenty-two thousand people a week and houses five hundred folks in the process of being rehabilitated. I take it all back. I can give the guy bad jokes and misattributed prayers. It's humbling to read everything this ministry is doing in LA while I'm just sitting on my sofa making snarky comments about other Christians. Well, as I like to say, human sin will fashion itself in endless variety.

THE ROUNDUP

Old Testament passages cited: Seemed like there must have been some, but they weren't cited.

New Testament passages cited: Ditto.

Cost of products offered: This one was a freebie.

Running total after 18½ hours: $7126.99

God: Rich and powerful daddy.

Thought for the show: Why is it that progressive Christians think we are the only ones who are "in solidarity with the poor"?

This Is Your Day with Benny Hinn
(*You can't go wrong combining gold lamé shoes and a Nehru jacket*)
11:30 p.m.

My guest Rick Kautz was ordained to the Episcopal priesthood in 1984 in the Diocese of Colorado and has served parishes in Colorado, Ohio, Florida, and now Indiana. He attended seminary at Nashotah House in Wisconsin. Prior to that he studied acting and comedy improv. He is the author of *A Labyrinth Year: Walking the Seasons of the Church*, published by Morehouse Books.

♦♦♦

The half-hour opens with a clip from *Praise the Lord*. MC Hammer sits on a garish sofa talking about how Jesus is better than nightclubs, which is, of course, a false dichotomy. I believe in Jesus *and* nightclubs, or even Jesus *in* nightclubs, but that's another story. Rick, having been here a mere two minutes, starts out with "Why would anyone have a sofa like that?" in reference to the ornate red and gold *PTL* sofa of righteousness.

"It looks like a bordello couch," Eric chimes in.

"Or a funeral home," Rick tops him.

"Or a bordello funeral home..." And we're off...

◆◆◆

Benny Hinn again.

Eric: "Can I hang out past my time slot? It's Benny Hinn!"

"I've already seen this today," I say. They both groan on my behalf, but I'm actually fine with it. I'm interested to see different reactions to the same show.

The guys are transfixed by Hinn's trance-inducing singing: "Jeeesss-susss." Hinn holds up his hands. "You're all I neeeeed, Jeeesssusss."

Rick offers, "This is very 'Wind beneath My Wings,' as though he's channeling Bette Midler," which is likely the first time Hinn's ever been accused of that particular feat of channeling.

"Is he wearing gold lamé shoes?" Eric asks.

"What else does one wear with a white Nehru jacket?" Rick explains.

"Jeeesssusss..." They cut from Hinn to the transfixed crowd, hands in the air, swaying back and forth, tears streaming down their faces.

"I would never allow myself to be filmed having a personal spiritual experience like that," Eric states.

"It's spiritually pornographic," I say, even though I'm not so sure what that means, but I'm simultaneously so tired and wired that certain neurons are no longer firing.

Five minutes in and Eric asks what's become *the* question: "Do you think that Benny Hinn believes that he's legit, that he's really doing God's work?"

Me: "Some people say that they don't think someone could actually believe they were fooling people and really live like that. Others say that maybe he's so deeply fallen into his own myth that he believes it himself." I say this, realizing though that it's not really an answer.

I don't know if there really is an answer to this. My gut says that Benny Hinn knows he's a charlatan, but in order to maintain this great thing he's got going for himself, he has to push that down into his emotional deep freeze in order to act like he's legit. The other question is whether or not there is actually good that comes from all of this Benny Hinn hooey.

Me: "He *is* doing something for people. If he was not having some sort of positive effect on people, then fifty thousand people wouldn't come to hear him, right?"

"Our God is so awesome," the "just healed" woman on screen says.

"Don't you agree," I add, "that we need to find a different adjective for the Almighty than the one that is most commonly used to describe one's pizza? 'Our pizza is awesome and our God is awesome.' "

Rick: "There's the song" ("Our God Is an Awesome God").

Me: "Which I think is embarrassing and makes me want to find a religion that doesn't involve cheesy praise music."

Rick: "I called Rich Mullens, and he says he always has to do that song and he doesn't really even like it."

Rick: "Who?" I ask.

"Rich Mullens, the author of that song. He's a great guy, well, was a great guy. He was killed."

"Was he killed for writing that song?" As soon as I say this, I regret it, but I've been watching TBN for almost nineteen hours now and have become a really bad person, like some weird Picture of Dorian Grey thing.

◆◆◆

Hinn is now in the studio talking to the camera about the love of God. "Jesus loves you. You are surrounded by his love. That's right, the very hairs on your head are numbered. He cares for you."

Eric: "Isn't that the second time we've heard that?"

True. I think they said that very same thing last hour. "Yeah, I've always thought that was weird, and people use that image all the time, but just because someone happened to know the number of the hairs on my head doesn't mean they necessarily have my back."

Eric: "Maybe if they knew the number of the hairs on your back . . . "

THE ROUNDUP

Old Testament passages cited: Zero.

New Testament passages cited: Zero.

Cost of products offered: $415.
    Taking the gospel to the ends of the earth: $360.
    Names of Jesus, book: $30.
    The Name of Jesus bracelet: $25.

Running total after 19 hours: $7541.99

Thought for this half-hour: Does he believe it?

Intermission
REFLECTION ON THE BLANK SCREEN
Do They Believe It?

S EVERAL QUESTIONS have consistently come up in conversations over the last few months of writing the book, but one tops the list: Do these people really believe what they are saying? This question is asked of me in practically every conversation I have about my experience of writing this book.

Do these folks believe what they are saying?

There seem to be two possible answers here: (1) They do, or (2) They don't.

If #1 is true, if Benny Hinn really believes without equivocation that he can heal people; if Paula White believes without hesitation that if you send her money you will get even more in return; if Rod Parsley can say without blinking that, well anything he says, then...what? There is no helpful "then" to that sentence. Then it's good for them? As someone who doesn't believe any of this for a moment, it's hard for me to imagine that they do either, but they may.

If #2 is true, and they really don't believe any of it, then the question becomes: Is that sort of fragmentation of the self possible to maintain? Can we really project a false self for that long without psychically necessitating an accommodation in the form of assimilation? Wouldn't one, in order to survive, have to *start* to believe it?

Therefore, I think they believe it because they don't believe it and the only way to maintain not believing it is to believe it.

Simple enough.

◆◆◆

Pastor Greg
(*Sublimated homoeroticism is funny*)
12:00 a.m.

My guest Sara Rosenau grew up an evangelical Quaker and accepted Jesus into her heart many times as a child. Now she's a member of the United Church of Christ (UCC) and in the ordination process with the Metro Denver Association of the UCC. Still, she sneaks off to worship with Episcopalians, Catholics, and Lutherans because she loves the Eucharist and all things high church. Sara is a graduate student of religion and social work. She lives with her partner, Kathleen, and her puppy, Finn, in Denver.

◆◆◆

Seth Donovan is a social worker in Denver who focuses on anti-oppression work with communities experiencing homelessness, human trafficking, and labor exploitation. She is interested in the church's role in various intersections of oppression. A lot of her thoughts, conversations, and energy lately have been invested in the internal to external movement of transformation and the nature of hope in our work for justice.

◆◆◆

Sara Rosenau and Seth Donavan show up just as *Pastor Greg* starts. They are my co-conspirators in the start of our new church. *Pastor Greg,* I recall from the first go round, is a Canadian situation comedy with Vacation Bible School–level production values and an absence of any discernable comedy. It's a Canadian situation, then. I'm certain it will be funnier this time, though, as last time I wasn't watching it with two lesbians and a gay man in my living room. And let's face it, that just makes everything funnier.

◆◆◆

The credits claim "Jesus Christ" as the executive producer.

Rick guffaws. "Is Emmanuel in the production booth? . . . 'Okay, cut to commercial.' "

The first scene starts with a terrible edit.

"Wow, Jesus sucks at this," Rick notices.

"That's the director. Jesus just funds it and signs the paperwork," I say.

"In all fairness," Rick adds, "most producers *are* Jewish."

◆◆◆

The show opens with the star: a middle-aged man wearing a wig so awful it begs the question: What could it possibly be covering up? From the pulpit Pastor Greg makes the announcement that he won't be able to preach tonight "because John and I have some pressing business to see to." The camera pans to a man in the congregation with a tight haircut, round metal glasses, and nice suit. He looks around, winks at the pastor, and gives him the thumbs up.

"Okay the guy on the left, so gay," claims Rick. "I could tell in the first frame."

The next scene finds Pastor Greg and the wire-framed guy lost in the woods trying to find a "fishing hole"; apparently that was their "important business."

"There's a definite *Deliverance* theme here — proving that . . . he really is gay." Rick's right. If a banjo starts playing be-da-ling-ding-ding-ding-ding-ding-ding my day will be complete.

Pastor Greg and the sissy boy run from a bear they encounter in the woods and end up stumbling upon some sort of restaurant. Walking in, they realize it's a bar. The guy at the door sports a handlebar moustache and leather jacket.

"Leather Bar," everyone in my living room says in unison.

There's even a dress code, so the leather daddy at the door hands Pastor Greg and John leather jackets and biker helmets, to which John responds "I can't wear this! It doesn't go with my ensemble! This is more Fall color and I'm a Summer."

We simply cannot stop laughing.

The Christian hijinks continue when the two are — seriously, I couldn't even wish for this — put in . . . a closet.

Who knew sublimated Christian homoeroticism in homemade sit com format could be so completely entertaining.

Seth: "This gay stuff couldn't possibly all be a coincidence."

To escape their closet prison they decide to crawl out the air duct only to fall back through the ceiling to the leather bar, one falling on top of the other. As John rolls off of Pastor Greg, he says "Well, that wasn't so bad."

There is no way this is accidental.

The storylines all wrap up and it's over before we know it.

I'm unsure how helpful the *Pastor Greg* show is to Christianity other than to weed out those with weak stomachs. How could all the super-gay stuff have gotten past them? It was purely delightful for us as delicious irony, but could the makers of the *Pastor Greg* show not have seen how very queer the entire show is?

Pastor Greg is actually a pastor named Greg who is the writer and director of *Pastor Greg* and creator of *www.pastorgreg.tv,* where he is telling us to go and buy Pastor Greg stuff. (Note to self: try to avoid becoming a megalomaniac closet case with a homemade sit com on TBN.)

◆◆◆

Thinking that whatever comes on next will be another TBN space filler and not anything terribly important, I head for the kitchen. Barely out of my seat I am startled to hear Seth and Sara simultaneously scream, literally scream, "Michael W. Smith!" Turning back to the TV, I see a 1990s music video complete with high-rise acid-wash jeans and power mullets. The music is unfamiliar to me but obviously not to my evangelically raised guests. Sara, still yelling, says "No way! This was my first concert ever!" "Me Too!" Seth matches. They high five each other and then start singing at the top of their lungs, "Find a place in this world, a place in this world" in that way that only those in touch with their own adolescent earnestness can muster.

I give them the pleading look that Eric gave me only an hour ago.

Rick: "Michael W. Smith is the Barry Manilow to Amy Grant's Bette Midler."

I have no idea what that means. Now I'm feeling a little out of the inner circle. I am just older enough to have missed out on the whole CCM (Contemporary Christian Music) thing.

"I've never even heard this song," I confess.

"You were definitely doing drugs by the time this came out," Sara mentions. "This was early 1990s."

Okay, she's right.

Seth: "I could watch Christian videos all night, dude."

The video ends with Michael W. Smith walking off into the sunset with the video girl, her feathered hair blowing in the wind.

Seth: "Finding your place in this world? I've just never actually seen this video. Apparently finding your place in this world is equivalent to finding a heterosexual relationship in the desert."

"Maybe that's why I'm so unfulfilled," Seth adds. "No one ever told me!"

THE ROUNDUP

Old Testament passages cited: Three.

New Testament passages cited: One.

Cost of products offered: $94.91.
    DVDs for seasons 1 and 2: $69.97.
    Pastor Greg T-shirts: $9.99.
    Christmas DVD: $14.95.

Running total after 19½ hours: $7636.90

Thought for this half-hour: The unintentionally funny is so funny.

The Ramp
(*Getting under the glory*)
12:30 a.m.

The Ramp: "A platform that takes you from one level to the next."

MTV for TBN. We're late enough in the night that TBN adults are fast asleep, but TBN teenagers are still going at it. The opening for *The Ramp* features a pleasingly bizarre mixture of techno music and Pentecostal ranting to an audience of teenagers revved up on hormones and praise bands.

"I believe in this room tonight," says a not in the least bit hip middle-aged woman preacher, "are the chosen warriors of God."

◆◆◆

The stage of what looks like a small nightclub is filled with teenage musicians and at least a dozen other teens in black T-shirts and camo pants standing without instruments whose role seems to be jumping up and down in a frenzy. As the Pentecostal preacher (Damon Thompson), hip and "relevant" with all his friendship bracelets, paces back and forth, he keeps passing a teenage boy behind him who's staring out from under a curtain of stringy brown hair with an intensity that is really disarming and slightly worrying. And he's swaying back and forth.

Seth: "If a kid came into my office looking like that, I'd assess him for a mental health hold."

The rock band comes back, along with the Pentecostal camo pants kids who do what I'm assuming is the improvised "chosen-warriors-of-God" dance.

"I was totally just doing that same dance at Lipgloss" (a Denver nightclub), says Seth, "but I'd never tell that I learned it all at youth group during Charismatic Church Camp."

"Yeah," I add. "That really gets the girls doesn't it?"

She laughs.

◆◆◆

"The music is awful," I can't help but say. "This is what I can't abide, bad music. Does *God* even like this?"

Sara laughs at my use of the word "abide." Biblical words are funny to us because we're such church geeks.

When the music ends the preacher comes back. Now he's talking smack about churches, which I actually think is kind of great. He's saying that churches have found ways to do church without God. If God shows up that's super, but if not, we've got a great band and an amazing coffee bar to offer. That's hysterical and he's right. "If you have a youth group without the power and presence of God, you've got a big waste of time on your hands. You have a glorified country club on your hands that's not producing anything."

Sara: "You know what we are supposed to be producing? Emotion. We must produce emotion at every single event. If emotion is not produced, the spirit is not present. I think that's the rubric."

She's got a point. I look up Damon Thompson. There are pictures on his website where every preacher has a look of such intensity on their faces that it appears like each of them is in the midst of a particularly difficult bowel movement. Scrolling through the pictures with this particular lens, I realize two things. One, this is the funniest thing in the whole world. Two, I am delirious.

Seth: "This is so much like what I grew up with, and my question was always: How do I *know* if the Spirit is in my life? I was completely tortured by that."

Sara: "Well, for them it looks like a really specific way; it's emotional and it's gyrating around."

I think a demonstration is not too much to ask at this point, but Sara declines.

◆◆◆

Thompson is claiming that pastors don't need to read another theological book. They need to get *under the glory*. "We don't need you to be cool; we need you *under the glory*. We don't need you to be funny; we need you *under the glory*." He paces in front of the intense kid repeating "get under the glory" about a dozen times. What does he mean by that anyhow?

Seth: "It's probably in Joshua somewhere, Israel being under God's glory."

Okay, so that's where the saying came from, but what does it mean on a functional level? How do you know if someone is "under the glory"? Is it a commitment to prayer and contemplation? Is it servant leaders who are committed not only to personal prayer but also to accountability and transparency in their leadership? Then I'm down with that. But if it really is claiming "supernatural power" to legitimize stuff you want to do anyway, which will bring glory (not to mention lots of cash) to yourself, then perhaps not.

I don't mind the idea of saying that God guides my leadership if everyone is really clear that it's always a messy and sometimes confusing mix of God's guidance and my saint/sinner self. I can try to discern God's will, but I hope I never claim to know what that is with certainty entirely on my own without the discernment of an entire community.

♦♦♦

This is all followed by more music and the gyrating Pentecostal haka dancing.

Seth: "This music sucks."

Me: "I can forgive bad theology more than bad music. There's just no excuse for that."

♦♦♦

Karen Weaton, the owner of *The Ramp*, comes on to implore folks: "You simply have to come visit *The Ramp*, where young people can experience the presence of God."

THE ROUNDUP

Old Testament passages cited: One.

New Testament passages cited: Seven.

Cost for one young person to experience the presence of God: $40.

Running total after 20 hours: $7676.90

God: Chooses warriors based on dance skills and how they look in camo pants.

Thought for this half-hour: Find the glory; get under it.

Virtual Memory
(Seriously? There's a Book of Jonah)
1:00 a.m.

It's *Virtual Memory*, a Bible knowledge game show for teenagers. I'm unsure why it's called virtual memory as opposed to *actual* memory. The set is a bit *Family Fued*-ish, with a team of teens lined up on each side and the host, a hyperactive little man, in the middle. The members of the teams take turns coming to the hyperactive little man's center console to answer questions.

Seth, Sara, and I were all three raised in some pretty Bible-heavy families, so this should be fun.

Feel free to play along at home.

Question #1: The book of Luke was written to what person?

Dorcus, Theophilus or...

Sara: "Theophilus."

Correct.

Question #2: Do you find the statement "Behold I stand at the door and knock," in Matthew, Acts, or Revelation?

Sara: "Matthew"

Answer: Revelation

Sara: "Really??"

Seth: *"If anyone hears my voice, yeah."*

Question #3: John the Baptist called some people a "brood of vipers." Did he say that to the sinners coming to be baptized, the Pharisees, or Jesus' disciples?"

Me: "Pharisees. Hey Seth, I know you know these. Bust it out, babe." She remains silent on the sofa.

Question #4: Name the members of the Trinity.

Protecting our pride, we all let this one go.

Question #5: He went from living in Pharaoh's house to tending sheep in the desert. Who was it?

"Moses," Sara says, rolling her eyes.

Question #6: Out of these three who was the only one to write a gospel and an epistle: John, Paul....

Me: "Or Ringo."

Answer: John (unless you ask a Bible scholar or seminary student; then it's the Johannine community).

Question #7: True or False. All the scribes and Pharisees did not believe in Jesus and wanted to get rid of him.

Sara: "False. What about Nicodemus?"

Question #8: In what book do you find the story of Jonah?

We are all stumped. We look at each other thinking, "No way, how can we not know this?"

Answer: The book of Jonah.

Yikes. A blush of humiliation comes over our faces, soon dispelled by belly laughing.

Question #9: Name two fruits of the Spirit

Me: "Faithfulness and self-control."

Question #10: Which of these conditions did Jesus not heal: blindness, missing leg, death?

"Missing leg," Sara says, "although I'd love to have seen that one."

Questions #11, 12 and 13: We can't understand what the hyper-active host is saying.

Question #14: Fill in this statement of Jesus: "I am the _____ of the world."

Sara: "Light. Seriously, this is all they've got?"

◆◆◆

All of a sudden I'm flashing back to junior high when our Church of Christ youth group would compete against other C of C youth groups in Bible trivia. "Did you guys have Bible Bowl when you were growing up?" I ask Seth and Sara. "You know, where the local youth groups would travel to each other's churches and compete in Bible quizzes?"

Seth and Sara simultaneously say, "Quiz Team!" I take that as a yes.

Then they both laugh the laugh of when you and another person simultaneously are reminded of something long forgotten from childhood, now loaded with irony. Things like Granimals, Underoos, Zoom, and if you were raised conservative evangelical, Quiz Team.

◆◆◆

A large slot of time in the *Virtual Memory* show goes to "thank" their sponsors. This includes lengthy descriptions of the following and the web address where you can buy them:

PC Study Bible software: $37.95–$449.95.

Heavenly Gear Athletic shoes with gold embroidered praying hands and "God Bless" stitched on the side: $49.95.

Vertical Music CDs: $14.95.

The scriptural references in this show were simply trivia content and are not used to support preaching or teaching so will be omitted from the totals.

THE ROUNDUP
Cost of products offered: 102.85 – $514.85.
Running total after 20½ hours: $7779.75
Thought for this half-hour: Brush up on that ol' Book of Jonah.

Bananas
(Christians don't need beer and the F-word to be funny)
1:30 a.m.

My guest Jerry H.: Jerry's story is a familiar one. Former bartender, stand-up comic, and mall Santa hears God's call to leave the bright lights of show biz and dedicate his life to doing the Lord's work. You've heard it a million times.

In addition to his work as a pastor at St. Andrew's United Methodist Church in Highlands Ranch, Colorado, Jerry currently serves on the board of directors for the Wesley Foundation.

Jerry has a passion for reaching out to those who have been told there is only "one way to do the God thing" and loves to be in dialogue with people who either don't trust organized religion or feel funny singing hymns they don't know.

◆◆◆

Seth and Sara are, of course, still here because it turns out that TBN is crack-like in its addictiveness.

Our friend Jerry arrives, which brings us great joy because Jerry is an LA comic turned Methodist pastor, and we love him. I grab him a beer as *Bananas,* the Christian comedy show, starts.

A middle-aged white guy stands alone on stage holding a mic stand; behind him is a brick wall. Everything about this says "comedy club" except the lack of the booze and the F-word, which are really the essential elements of comedy, when it comes right down to it.

Aping the cliché comedy club opening lines, Jerry says in his best comic voice, "*So anyone here saved? Raise your hands if you love the Lord Jesus Christ? Great to have you here tonight.* Every Christian comic I've seen just does their regular stand-up act and then at the end they throw in a scripture verse. It's a total racket."

◆◆◆

Ken Davis is introduced as the first comic. He does a fairly entertaining bit asking if anyone has ever had his or her airbag deploy. "It's not like on TV. They make it *look* like fun because they show it like some slow motion marshmallow. But it's not like that. You don't see it coming; you don't hear it coming. All you know is that your nose hurts worse than it's ever hurt in its life." We all laugh.

"When I was growing up there was no such thing as a seat belt," Davis continues. Jerry and I look at each other. "If he does this . . . " Jerry swings his arm all the way out to his right. "Exactly," I say. Of course Davis does. "Hack," Jerry and I say in unison. That whole mom's-arm-as-seatbelt thing is as hack as "I could tell you, but then I'd have to kill you," or the entire topic of airline food. It's been done. To death.

"What makes him a Christian comic?" Seth asks. Ding ding ding! The question of the day. When something is called "Christian," what does this mean? These people aren't even doing Bible-based material. The irony is that in my twenties when I was doing stand-up and was personally not even the least bit Christian, I did loads of biblical material — like how embarrassed we'd all be if we found out the Bible was really just a two-thousand-year-old supermarket tabloid. "And God said to the people: Go forth and worship Oprah who has in this very year lost forty pounds on the South Beach Diet." I used the stage to poke fun at my own evangelical upbringing: "When I was growing up all the other kids in Sunday school had illustrated Bibles, you know . . . pictures of Jesus. Yeah, I had a scratch-and-sniff Bible. Seriously, ever smelled a leper?" There's a reason I did stand-up only for three years. It turns out I'm not that funny.

Jerry decides to call the TBN prayer line. He calls but only gets a message. "My call cannot be completed? What does that mean for me? What if I had a barrel in my mouth?"

He tries again. "My call will be answered in the order it was received?" He hangs up in defeat.

"They've probably blocked my number by now," I explain.

◆◆◆

Seth takes her leave. And then there were three. Three people watching bad "Christian" stand-up at 1:45 a.m. in my living room. Except that rather than stand-up we're now having to watch a between-comics interlude; Davis teaching people rope tricks in a mall somewhere. "Is this like, *rope ministry*?" I ask.

Rather than try to figure it out, I start talking about something completely unrelated because my thought patterns have become a bit random, and all I can think about is how funny the Bible is. "In my preaching class last week," I offer, "we talked about texts that never come up in the lectionary, like Balaam's ass" (a story in the twenty-second chapter of the book of Numbers involving a talking ass, and not the kind one gets from too much Taco Bell). "Or," Jerry adds, "dashing babies' heads against the stone" (the end of Psalm 137). "Kinda hard to preach off that."

"So," I continue, "the thing in the class was to talk about how we'd preach this Balaam's ass text, to which I replied, 'I'm pretty sure that's what puppet ministries are for.'"

"Yeah," Jerry explains, "that's why God made clown ministry: for texts like Leviticus 15, which is all about stuff like sperm and menstruation. I know that when I have to lead devotionals before a meeting or event I like to say, 'Before we pray let's open up the Word to Leviticus 15.' That just really sets the tone for church council."

◆◆◆

So *Bananas* has produced some genuine Christian stand-up, though just in my living room.

"Hey, you guys are funnier than this guy Ken," Sara says.

"Yeah, and we're at least talking about scripture. What makes this guy a Christian comic anyway?" I ask. Ding ding ding.

Sara: "I think it's that if they know he's Christian then they feel safe."

"But safe from what?" I ask, "beer and blasphemy?" (Note to self: start a conversation group called Beer and Blasphemy.)

Sara's laughing her tushy off even though Jerry and I aren't that funny. TBN has lowered the funny barometer to the point that Jerry and I sound hilarious. "Can you guys come to Iliff (the seminary we all went to or still go to) and do a comedy show?"

"Yeah, um ... not even for eternal salvation," insists Jerry.

Cost of products offered: $89.97 for three seasons of *Bananas* on DVD.

Running total after 21 hours: $7869.72

Thought for this half-hour: I should challenge all my other pastor friends to incorporate Leviticus 15 into their sermons for next week.

Prize: Fabergé-style egg.

Xtreme Life
(*How would Jesus surf?*)
2:00 a.m.

Disclaimer: The images you are about to witness are performed by pro athletes. Don't try any of these stunts at home.

◆◆◆

Rad. Awesome. Off the hook. No it's not the evangelical God we're talking about, but the skateboard, motocross, and surfing stunts that open *Xtreme Life,* dedicated to Christian extreme sports. While I'd love to say this involves lions and a Roman coliseum — because boy would *that* help keep me awake — the show is simply an extreme sports show, but I'm guessing the hosts and athletes are Christian.

"So today I've watched Christian talk shows, Christian news, Christian MTV, Christian stand-up comedy, and later there will be Christian cartoons." I tell my guests, "Now we have Christian extreme sports. I guess you could pretty much slap the label Christian on any genre of show by praying at the end and — poof! — there's a whole market lining up to consume your product. What kind of 'Christian' show could we pitch that is just a low-budget copy, but at the end we pray?"

"Porn." Jerry says without missing a beat,

"Hey, that Leviticus 15 bit might come in real handy," agrees Sara.

◆◆◆

The only thing that keeps us from continuing down this road of suggesting what TBN "adult entertainment" might look like are the images on our screen, which are pornographic in their own right, but this is voyeurism of a whole different order. Young men, one after the other, wipeout while doing motorcycle stunts. This feels like one step away from a Christian snuff film, a long neglected genre in the entertainment branch of the Christian-Industrial complex. But I'm assuming these boys live. The Christian death metal music they play in the background adds to the "extreme" nature of the show.

Jerry begins to question how this might be a helpful evangelism tool if one were to show these clips to someone interested in the faith. "Wanna see some cool Christians? See that guy right there? [Guy pulls a wheelie gone bad and his bike ends up on top of him.] He's Christian. So is that guy [spinning donuts, his bike spins out from under him]."

"Jerry," Sara explains, "it's okay, because *God* is with them." The next guy is thrown completely off his bike and into a wall of tires at full speed, his face hitting pavement.

"Except maybe that guy," Jerry says. Yeah, unfortunately I think God might have sneezed right there.

◆◆◆

A speed metal Christian video comes on. It's very dark. The lead guitarist, taking his power stance, swings his long dreadlocks around. This is pretty far from Paul Crouch Jr. on the ornate *PTL* set, and I have to admit I far prefer this to schmaltz. There's a reason this is on at two in the morning; the programming skews young. I'm almost ashamed to admit that I prefer it to anything else that's come on today. Except limbless day on *PTL*, which was euphoric. Part of me resents the fact that I like the programming so obviously marketed to my demographic; am I so easily marketed to?

Jerry, Sara, and I are becoming disenchanted with the "male adolescent testosterone I'm-invincible-and-can-do-dangerous-stuff-because-I-believe-in-God" stunts.

◆◆◆

I'm vaguely aware of how downhill the discourse has gone since this morning. Wasn't I actually thinking about theology and biblical interpretation earlier today? Now after twenty-one hours I've digressed to ass jokes, but, in all fairness, I'm not sure that could be avoided.

◆◆◆

The *Xtreme Life* host interviews the producer of a big wave surfing film about surfing and Jesus, in that order. Not a lot of theological sophistication here, just the standard "Jesus wants to be in a relationship with you" stuff. Which makes me wonder: Which came first, the Jesus is my boyfriend praise music or the Jesus is my boyfriend theology? The host then turns to the camera: "Right now if you want, you can start this personal relationship with Jesus Christ," after which a message comes on the screen: "Want the gift of eternal life? Check out our website for more information."

An extreme sports website that promises eternal life proves too much for us to resist, so we take the bait.

There is nothing about salvation on the home page.

Here are the sidebar links in order:

"Home": nothing.

"Store": loads of DVDs to buy, no eternal life to be found anywhere.

"News": nada.

"Need prayer?": just a prayer request form to fill out.

"Watch now": nope.

"Truth": this must be it. Under the area "questions" on the "truth" link is information about the *Xtreme Life* show. You may choose to click on a video of the host quoting John 3:16, but that's about it.

"Donate": by this time we know what this is about.

"XLinternational": global missions stuff.

"Where to watch": obviously not.

Sara is at this point laughing hysterically. "I wanna get saved and this website is not helping me at all."

"Partner": more fundraising stuff.

"Contact": email info.

So there are plenty of opportunities to give them money but how's an extreme girl to get eternal life on this website?

◆◆◆

Next we're treated to a montage of stunt motorcycle wipeouts, moto-cross wipeouts, and surfing wipeouts, and then a scripture on the screen: "Who is he that even the wind and the waves obey him?" (Mark 4:41).

The host comes back on to guide people again to their website, where you can find "ministry tools," like DVDs, that "tell the real-life stories of the world's top athletes whose lives changed after having an encounter with Jesus Christ." At the words "Jesus" and "Christ," the images changed like lightning from surfers to a very bloody crucifixion, for less than one second, and then back to their website. Sara and Jerry lose it.

"What was *that?*" Sara asks.

Jerry offers, "You think motocross and surfing is extreme? Try crucifix-ion! Here's the latest extreme sport: we nail you to a cross, drop you in the ocean, and you surf in *on* the cross. It's balsa wood, okay?"

To which I add, "Basically what you need to ask yourself is 'How Would Jesus Surf?'"

Sara tops us both: "The crucifixion portrayed on our show was under-taken by the son of God, a trained professional. Do not try to crucify yourself at home."

We're all going to hell.

THE ROUNDUP

Old Testament passages cited: Zero.

New Testament passages cited: Two.

Cost of products offered: $39.90 for refined DVD, *Best of Xtreme Life.*

Running total after 21½ hours: $7909.62

Jesus: Wants to be in relationship with surfers, dude.

Thought for this half-hour: All organizations promising salvation on their websites should deliver on the home page.

Team Impact
(*Jesus of Nazareth: Lamb of God, or cagefighter?*)
2:30 a.m.

My guest Andie Lyons has a hard time coming to conclusions, insofar as her personal religious beliefs are concerned. This is a deep and lasting familial trait that was instilled in her as a child. Baptized in an Episcopal cathedral, toted around to various places of worship — including but not limited to a Mormon church, the Church of Religious Science, the Krishna Consciousness temple and restaurant, and various mainline Christian churches — Andie currently pays homage to this hodge podge perspective by attempting to integrate Unitarian Universalism and Lutheran theology. In addition to her dizzying religious life, Andie is also a professionally queer lady who gets paid to create safe spaces for LGBTQ youth. She enjoys pulling pranks on her girlfriend Sara, writing zines, making up ridiculous dance moves, and taking her small menagerie of animals on tours of Denver's warehouse districts.

◆◆◆

Andie is a no-show. I call and wake her up. She's upset about falling asleep and vows to get here as soon as she can. To miss *Team Impact* would devastate her, for it is the pinnacle of TBN weirdness. This is what I've been waiting for. It's 2:30 in the morning; I am hopped up on Diet Coke and chocolate like nobody's business, and there are two (soon to be three) people in my living room watching a show dedicated to steroids for the savior. If over the last twenty-one and a half hours I've questioned what makes these shows Christian per se, I will get no answers here. To imply (as this show does) that the ability of enormous steroidal men to break cinder blocks using stage karate is granted by the power of the Holy Spirit is theologically far reaching even for people less prone to cynicism than myself.

◆◆◆

On my TV hip-hop music (I'm assuming it's "Christian") pounds as several musclebound men in tank tops stand in front of a large banner reading "Abundant Life Christian Center." One of them breaks a dozen or so cinder blocks with his bare arms (Praise God).

"You know what that is right there?" Jerry asks, "Abundant living."

A montage of images follow. Big men breaking blocks of ice, bending steel bars, karate chopping blocks of wood. This allows Jerry to make a rather keen theological observation: "All these guys pray. All these guys break stuff. Is that a coincidence? I don't think so."

◆◆◆

I've zoned out thinking about the last couple of hours of TBN. The programming, especially the game show, the MTV thing, the extreme sports show, and now this body builder stuff is obviously geared toward young people. It all feels like Christian propaganda aimed at church kids, a false notion of what will keep young people in church. Perhaps the idea is that if being Christian looks just like the culture, then that will keep the culture from luring our kids away. If we are going to get them not to leave church, we have to make Christian stuff just like secular stuff.

◆◆◆

On screen, a bodybuilder testifies, "Sitting in my car one day I turned on the radio. There was a song playing from the 1980s called "I Want to Know What Love Is." It was a secular song; it had nothing to do with God. . . ."

"Much like bodybuilding and breaking stuff," I interject.

The testimony is followed by another montage of Team Impact feats of strength. "Ladies and Gentlemen," an amped up announcer voice à la Monster Truck Rally proclaims, "We are Team Impaaaaact. Standing on faith tonight let's give it up for the King of Kings and Lord of Lords, the one, the only, the Risen Warriooooooor!"

Are they talking about Jesus? Is he a cage fighter or the Lamb of God? If ever there was a cross-denying tribute to a theology of glory, it would be Team Impact. As is the case with the rest of TBN, the scandal of Jesus' birth, life, teachings, death, and resurrection are ignored entirely in favor of a Jesus-as-Rambo theology; here the Lord just kicks ass and takes names, much like the freakishly muscular Team Impact guys. Taking one's Christology from a couple of chapters of Revelation (ignoring the central Christ image, that of the Lamb who was slain) rather than the gospels is baffling to me. I recently saw an "inspirational" self-mocking emerging church poster. The word "incarnational" rested below an image of a heavily tattooed guy wearing a crown of thorns made of barbed wire. The caption read "What would Jesus do? I'm pretty sure he'd do stuff I think is cool." We all wish to make Christ in our own image because the truth of a God who dies is too much. We'll believe anything but that, and if that anything happens to bring us power and victory and glory then all the better.

A man with twenty-two-inch biceps bends a frying pan into a burrito shape with his bare hands, which makes me admit, "You know scripturally speaking you can't actually bend a skillet *without* the Holy Spirit. I think that's in Ephesians."

"So," I ask, "are these guys just constantly looking around their homes thinking, 'What in here could I break for the Lord?' Their wives are throwing their bodies between their husbands and their cookware. 'Please, Steve, not the Calphalon. Maybe the Lord needs you to break a socket wrench today.'"

Jerry reminds me that it is God, and not us, deciding which household items need to be broken on the Lord's behalf. Such piety.

"Jerry, now that I think about it, right now when I opened your beer for you, I felt a little victorious in the Lord just doing that."

We try to focus again on the enormous man giving his testimony.

"When I got saved," he says "I got radically transformed."

"How?" Sara asks.

"Mostly in the triceps area. You should have seen my flaccid triceps. But now with the Lord Jesus Christ in my life cinder blocks everywhere fear me."

I can't stop.

He continues by telling of his mother's drug, alcohol, and child abuse. When he "got saved" he went back home and tearfully told her that she was forgiven. Here I finally see Christ in this show; I can't be cynical about forgiveness. In Luther's small catechism he teaches that where there is forgiveness of sins there is life and salvation. I think that's right. Forgiveness: *there* is true strength and true power.

◆◆◆

Responding to the weird Christology we're exposed to, we turn to discussing Trinitarian theology. "So is God one-sixth human?" I ask. Baffled, Jerry and Sara look at me like I'm Steven Hawking. "Seriously. If Jesus is one third of the Trinity and he himself is one half human, then God is one-sixth human, right?" They say nothing. Perhaps I should not be trying to operate heavy theology right now.

◆◆◆

Andie arrives. "I was dead asleep, but I couldn't miss this."

"Yeah, this guy just broke a bat over his crotch for Jesus." Jerry fills her in: "This is what being saved is all about."

Andie and her Super Big Gulp join us on the sofa of judgment. I'm growing weary of my own cynicism. That's why Andie's here to take over. We don't call her Judge-y Smurf for nothing.

Andie has actually seen Team Impact live, which doesn't really make sense as she's Unitarian. I've always assumed her interest in Christian bodybuilders who demonstrate feats of strength for the Lord was primarily anthropological in nature. "You guys know more about the New Testament than me," she admits. "Is there something in there about Jesus breaking stuff?"

Jerry answers first, "I will tear down the temple and rebuild it in three days. Now, if these guys can put this stuff back together, then that's impressive."

◆◆◆

I ask Andie if she'd be willing to call the number on the screen and ask them to pray that she too might break some stuff for the Lord.

Sara offers, "What about, 'I'm trying to stay awake to watch this show. Would you pray that I make it?'"

Andie backs down. "I think Jerry should do it. Jerry, call and ask them to pray that *you* might break some stuff."

Jerry: "I break things all the time."

Andie: "But is it for the Lord?"

Jerry: "It is now."

THE ROUNDUP

Thought for this half-hour: Does a God who can raise the dead really need Team Impact to break stuff for him?

Children's Heroes of the Bible
(I've become a monster)
3:00 a.m.

The transition between *Team Impact* and a show of animated Bible stories seems a bit abrupt. But the bouncy theme song helps: "Great Stories, Bible Stories, Stories that are true..."

◆◆◆

After the intro, the words "The Story of Elijiah" appear on the screen. (The title page indicates that this was produced in 1978 by the America Lutheran Church. This primitive cartoon is the sole representation of Lutheranism on TBN.)

Sara, having been here for three hours instead of one, is trying to leave.

"An Elijah cartoon?" she says as she turns around. "That *is* a great Bible story." I have a feeling she's staying. "Are they going to show that thing where he lies on top of a dead boy?" Yep, she sits back down.

"Regardless, I read the book. It was better," Jerry adds, "but I have to say I love the fact that according to this cartoon series, all the stories of the Bible are about white people."

Jerry then poses a valid question, "Maybe it's just me, but what kid is getting up at three o'clock, raring to go, saying, 'Okay, I'm ready to watch some stuff—either Barney or the Wiggles or Elijah.'"

"Homeschoolers?" I offer.

◆◆◆

The primatively animated story we're watching is about when Elijah prophesied to King Ahab that there would be no rain until the people heeded the word of the Lord. There were few people who still loved God, among them a little boy and his widowed mother. God told Elijah to go to the widow Joanna and her boy, who would feed him. Anyway, long story short, Sara and I are dying to see how they deal with the part of the story in which the boy dies and Elijah lies on top of him and places his mouth on the boy. Grown men who lie on top of dead boys while kissing them is likely inappropriate in any time or culture.

We are disappointed. The 1978 animated Elijah simply kneels next to the boy, placing his hands on the boy's abdomen, and prays. To verify what actually happens in the text, Sara grabs the Bible that sits on my sofa for just that reason.

I'd love to be in on that production meeting, "Well, when we initially decided to animate the Elijah story we did not realize it ends with Elijah lying on top of the boy."

They are right of course: the Bible is no book for children. Noah's ark? Let's decorate all our children's nurseries with the apocalyptic story of how God killed every living thing on earth except eight humans and two of each animal. That is a text of terror, not whimsy.

She looks it up: "1 Kings 17:21, he lay upon the child three times, but Nadia I think you made up the mouth thing up."

The next Elijah story is what Mark George (the Hebrew Bible scholar of 1:30 p.m.–2:30 p.m. fame) calls the Annie-get-your-gun contest between Elijah and the prophets of Baal. "Everything your God can do mine can do better."

They set up altars to each of their gods to see which god would send fire down to burn it. The Baal dudes got bupkis, but when it was Elijah's turn he upped the ante by pouring water on his altar before God indeed set fire to it.

◆◆◆

For the next three minutes, something unexplainable comes on as a space filler.

Rhyme Time, a computer-animated short, offers three animated rocks singing bad fake rap about listening to your mom and dad, which makes *Ice Ice Baby* feel downright gangster. When deciding what inanimate object to animate I'm sure the idea of rocks seemed plausible at the time, but the result is more like singing blocks of jello. I'm not sure why, but after twenty-two hours of TBN I find myself deeply disturbed by this and need to step away from the TV for a minute. Fortunately reinforcements show up. The two people signed on for the last shift are from the Urban Servant Corps, a Denver-based Lutheran Peace Corps thing. Here's what's weird: I've never met them before. The first time we meet is as I welcome them into my living room at 3:30 in the morning to watch Christian cartoons.

◆◆◆

In the "Verse of the Day" segment, a seven-year-old blond girl slides down a slide, looks into the camera, and says, "My favorite verse is 'I can do all things through Christ who strengthens me' (Phil. 4:13)."

"That's totally hack," I say, and then I realize that I've become some sort of monster, mocking a child for not coming up with a more obscure verse to offer as her favorite. I seriously don't like myself.

THE ROUNDUP

Cost of products offered: $0.

Running total after 22½ hours: $7909.62

Kids, even strange little homeschooled ones who watch Christian TV at 3:00 a.m., are not doing so with their MasterCard in their little hands.

Thought for this half-hour: The Bible is not exactly the stuff from which to glean children's stories; this is part of what makes it great reading.

BJ's Teddy Bear Club
(*Dancing poultry time!*)
3:30 a.m.

My guest Scott Piebenga is a skateboarder living in Denver. He was raised in a Christian Reformed Church in western Michigan. His favorite part about church is drinking coffee and shaking hands.

◆◆◆

My guest Amy: I was born and raised in the ELCA tradition, deviated, tried evangelism, balanced out, and now consider myself generally spiritual with an emphasis in Christianity. What "spiritual" means for me changes daily. Right now I am a full-time volunteer, living in intentional community and helping low-income women transition from tough life situations into self-sufficiency and employment.

◆◆◆

The title alone of the next show is making me wonder if I'm going to make it. It's *BJ's Teddy Bear Club*. No, seriously, it's *BJ's Teddy Bear Club*.

"*BJ's Teddy Bear Club* educates and informs children between the ages of one and five about letters, colors, and numbers through a lovable animated Teddy Bear. . . ."

I feel like the age demographic TBN is pitching to has gone from sixties and seventies (preaching and *PTL*) to fifties ("news" shows and that thing on menopause) to people in their thirties and forties (sit coms and stand-up) to twenties (extreme sports) to teens (*The Ramp*, *Team Impact*) to school-age kids (Bible stories) and, finally, toddlers. I too have from yesterday morning until now regressed into a basically preverbal state. I was so serious earlier in the day with my theological commentary. Then I became disengaged, then giggly, and now . . . BJ's Teddy Bear Bible stories: Joseph and his brothers.

A brown little animated teddy bear is reading toddlers a Bible story about the youngest son of a big family who was sold into slavery when his older brothers got jealous of his new coat. "That wasn't very nice," BJ Bear says in his squeaky teddy bear voice. (Amy adds that the coat shown in the cartoon was neither amazing nor Technicolor.) The story continues as the blond-haired, blue-eyed, Egyptian wife of "Joseph's boss" has him thrown into prison for not noticing her, "and that's no fun," according to the bear. I start to think about how great a Teddy Bear Study Bible might be. Rather than exegetical notes on the original Greek, there would be comments like, "Ouch, that's gotta hurt," when Jesus is flogged, and "Yippie!" at the resurrection.

The pharaoh (blue-eyed himself) sounds strangely like Jackie Gleason.

The squeaky teddy bear voice is agitating me to the point that I can't actually keep watching without risking a stroke or something equally debilitating. But I'm close enough to 5:00 a.m. and that blessed moment when I get to go to bed that I don't want to sabotage myself by drinking anymore coffee, so I get up and walk outside for a minute. As I turn to close the door, I'm amused to see four people in my living room at almost four in the morning watching Teddy Bear Bible stories. I inhale the fresh air as though having just surfaced from being pulled under a tidal wave.

When I reenter my living room, there's a children's song, "Dance like the Animals" playing while animated poultry "dance."

Jerry: "Do you find yourself wondering if they just simply run out of God talk, and they think, 'Screw it. Just put some chickens on there.'"

"All I know is," Amy adds, "now that I've seen poorly animated dancing chickens, I'm ready to give my life to Christ."

I'm so completely overstimulated right now that I'm wishing our house had come with a sensory deprivation tank.

THE ROUNDUP

Old Testament passages cited: Story of Joseph, kind of.

New Testament passages cited: Zero.

Cost of products offered: $0.

Running total after 23 hours: $7909.62

Thought for this half-hour: N/A.

Greatest Heroes and Legends of the Bible
(Through the rabbit hole)
4:00 a.m.

Once again an old white man addresses the TBN audience from a well-appointed mahogany and leather study, only this time it is Charlton Heston, beloved actor and activist.

(Andie and Jerry both leave.)

Heston is introducing us to the story of Jonah (which I now can say with confidence is found in the book of Jonah).

"If there is one recurring theme in the Bible," Heston tells us in that stentorian voice, "it's that God is everywhere and is aware of every human thought."

Okay, that's creepy.

That's the theme? Really? Not that God is abounding in steadfast love? No, God-as-Big-Brother is the overriding theme. This God has a surveillance system to die for — and did. Kevin Maly, in a sermon I heard once, said that God would rather die than be in the sin-accounting business anymore. So that's what the cross is about.

For some unexplainable reason, this reminds me that I promised to wake up my kids to watch the last show with me. They actually are so TV-deprived that they spring out of bed eager for the opportunity to consume the heavily rationed media. Of course the fact that what they are about to watch is Charlton Heston's *Greatest Heroes of the Bible* is as if they were deprived candy and as a treat I tossed sugar-free diabetic chocolate into their hungry little baby-bird mouths.

Heston recalls the story of Jonah, and then the screen depicts the cartoon version of the same story. I'm unsure what purpose Heston serves other than to possibly keep the over-seventy set interested while they watch TBN at four in the morning with their homeschooled great-grand-children. That's just my best guess.

◆◆◆

Here's the gist: Jonah is an Israelite whose mortal enemies are the Assyrians (especially the town of Nineveh). (Scott: "I'm confused by the obscure ethnic conflict that I know nothing about.") Well, we all are confused, but the important thing is that the Assyrians have destroyed Jonah's village many times. God tells Jonah to go to Nineveh to bring warning of their destruction if they do not repent and turn to God. Jonah thinks this is a lousy idea.

"Because," I add, "the most important thing to remember about God is that he hates everyone I hate."

Scott agrees, "Yeah, I mean Nineveh is in Assyria, and they hate those guys. That's a rough spot to be in."

I agree. "It'd be like God saying to me, 'Go forth to Ann Coulter and warn her that she left the water on in the bathroom,' and I'd be like 'Forget that; she deserves it.'"

◆◆◆

In order to try to get out of the whole warning Nineveh thing, Jonah gets on a ship heading the opposite direction. At sea the ship is threatened by wild storms; when the crew realizes that this is due to Jonah, they throw him overboard. As Jonah panics, sinking to the depths of the ocean (Amy sings, "Under the sea, under the sea, darling it's better, Down where it's wetter..."), God sends a big fish to swallow him up. (Scott: "If nothing else, it's a great lesson on digestion".)

I'm vaguely aware that my stomach is killing me. Twenty-four hours of coffee and cheese puffs, Diet Coke and candy could have something to do with it, but I'm unwilling to say for sure. I just need not to be watching something right now that is focused on stomachs, but I'm stuck for the moment.

Jonah is in the fish's belly for quite some time before being spit out onto the shores of — you guessed it — the city of Nineveh. But while still in the belly of the fish, things get weird (in the cartoon version that is). And here in my living room version I seem to be slipping in and out of wakefulness. As Jonah floats in the fish belly water, his reflection talks to him.

"Ill never get out of here" Jonah says.

"Make the best of it," answers his reflection. "I spent years in this sorry place."

No longer the chisled-face cartoon Jonah, now it is Paula White's perfectly botoxed mug looking back at me. "I'll never get out of here," I repeat. "Just offer your love gift, plant your best seed, and it'll all be over."

"That's all it took this whole time? I could have gone back to Kansas at any time during this 23.75 hours if I had just given my best love offering?"

I'm jostled back awake when my head falls down to my chest. I'm back in my huge living room chair, a kid on each side, Jonah on the TV. I glance at the clock hoping I dozed off for awhile, but unmercifully it's still 4:40 a.m.

"What are you talking about?" Jonah asks the image facing him "You're my reflection; you go where I go."

"Oh sure," his reflection answers. "When I first came here I was just like you, but I'd be careful of that stuff if I were you," referring to the stomach fluid he just fell into.

"What's it made of?"

"Hate." His reflection claims, "If you're not careful it will eat away at you until you plain ol' disappear."

"But it's not hate," I tell the Paula White face in the water. "It's theological and cultural criticism."

"Maybe it starts that way, but . . . "

"Wait," I say, sensing something is wrong. "What do you mean? You started out like me?"

She answers by saying, "Can I have some orange juice?"

Paula disappears as I become aware of my seven-year-old son sitting next to me in the big chair. "Yeah, honey, go ahead."

I look at the clock. 4:42 a.m. This is never going to end.

"But I've learned my lesson, at least I think I have," says Jonah.

Suddenly snakes surface from the belly waters and taunt him, "It's too late. You're one of us now."

"NOoooooo," Jonah protests. I surrender while snakes — the heads of which are Benny Hinn, Joel Osteen, Joyce Meyer, Paul Crouch Jr., and that weird psychotic boy from *The Ramp* — pull me under the waters of hate until I jolt out of my chair.

Jonah follows through with his mission, albeit begrudgingly. The Ninevites repent, God spares them, etc., etc.

Is TBN my Nineveh? I don't want God to bless this ridiculous "ministry," which stands for so much that I can't stand.

I can't think anymore, hear anymore, see anymore. I take a picture of me and the kids and then thank Amy and Scott as they leave into the black of the November morning. The kids crawl back into bed, and I do the same. The blessedness of sleep comes — but slowly, first having to push aside images of body builders and prosperity preachers, cartoons and menopausal evangelicals.

◆◆◆

I wake from a dreamless sleep five hours later. As I wander into my living room, a thought enters my mind before my will can do anything about it. *I wonder what's on TBN.*